Praise

Bryan Heathman's marketing acumen is unparalleled in the new world of publishing. The step-by-step guide #1 Best Seller offered valuable insights about how to maximize sales for our book launch.

- Robert A. Dickinson, Author
of *Score College Scholarships*

Bryan is brilliant, the material is timely, targeted, and based on years of success. The book is a winner to be sure. If you want to not just get published but get sales as well, you now hold the keys to success in your hand.

Buy it, read it, do it!

- Chris Majer, Founder, The Human Potential Project and author of *The Power of Transformation*

I find Bryan Heathman's wealth of knowledge in marketing fascinating as he's constantly thinking on how to spread the word to vast audiences.

- Dan Lewis, Retired ABC Television News Anchor

For the first-time Bryan Heathman publicly shares the inside secrets of what it takes to be massively successful as an author in today's publishing landscape. If you want to change the world, this is your playbook.

- **Dan Waldschmidt**, Bestselling author *of EDGY Conversations*

Once again Bryan gives you the tools to cut your learning curve by at least 50%. Brilliant!

- **Dr. Sheila Murray Bethel**, National Bestselling author of *Making A Difference*

Bryan Heathman is the perfect person to offer book marketing strategies having published hundreds of speakers and authors. His advice is rock solid.

- **Patricia Fripp**, CSP, CPAE. Past President, National Speakers Association.

Bryan Heathman is a man on a mission...a mission to help others to have greater success. He is an expert marketer and has helped many people to create amazing book projects. He has great ideas and great insights that can help you have great success with your book. Read this book and then go to work on what he recommends! You will be glad you did!

- **Dr. Willie Jolley**, Bestselling author of *A Setback Is A Setup For A Comeback* & *An Attitude of Excellence*

Writing books is pure pleasure! Marketing them can be agony. Without an adequate plan, authors don't stand a chance in today's flooded book market. Buy this book so you can sell your own, and get to write another one!

-**Joseph Castleberry,** President, Northwest
University and author of *Forty Days of Christmas*

Finally! A roadmap to separate the pretenders from the performers. With over 100 tactics to implement, Bryan unpacks the steps that reveal a 'behind the scenes' look to becoming a Bestselling author.

- **Scott Hogle**, #1 Bestselling author of *Persuade*

Made for Success Publishing
P.O. Box 1775
Issaquah, WA 98027

ISBN 978-1-64146-287-7 (Hardback)
ISBN: 978-1-64146-346-1 (Paperback)
LCCN: 2018905008

Library of Congress Cataloging-in-Publication data

Heathman, Bryan
#1 Best Seller: Book Marketing... Reinvented
pages. Cm
1. BUSINESS & ECONOMICS / Marketing / General
2. LANGUAGE ARTS & DISCIPLINES / Authorship
3. LANGUAGE ARTS & DISCIPLINES / Publishing

Printed in the United States of America

#1 BEST SELLER

BOOK MARKETING...
REINVENTED

Bryan Heathman

Contents

Introduction

The Book Marketing Journey

THE task of marketing a book has changed dramatically, and authors often find it a challenge to keep up with the latest methods to promote their book. In speaking with highly successful authors, they share that the marketing tactics they employed years ago are simply ineffective today.

To address the rapidly changing field of book marketing, this book is designed to help authors simplify and organize their book marketing activities.

After the hard work of getting a book ready to commercialize, this is the time when successful authors turn their attention to book marketing. I like to say that writing a book is 10% of the effort. Getting the word out is 90%. The sheer fact that these words are in your hands means you are part of the top 2% of authors who understand this dynamic and are willing to do the work which has been paved by many successful authors before you.

To be successful, you must be willing to do the
things today others won't do in order to have
the things tomorrow others won't have.

~Les Brown

Knowing when to do marketing activities at the right time is a key to a great book launch. Book marketing activities typically begin 2-months prior to launch and last up to 3-months post-launch. This is the time when the author is active in the media to spread the message and make the public aware that the book is available in retailers.

In studying this marketing system on effective book marketing activities, you are equipping yourself with the knowledge to become a best-selling author. For each individual, this system will put you in a position to organize your campaign, establish what makes sense to do yourself and what to delegate to others.

At the end of this book is a framework called the *Book Marketing Prioritization System*. With the understanding of your marketing options in the pages to follow, coupled with the *Book Marketing Prioritization System*, your future as a published author is bright indeed.

1

The Book Marketing Formula

ONCE upon a time, an author would write their book and the world would flock to read it. Those times have changed, given the sheer enormity of new books entering the marketplace each year. With all the demands on a reader's attention coupled with hundreds of thousands of new book choices to sort through each year, authors need to capture the attention of their audience in order to break through in this crowded marketplace.

Planning a book launch is the starting place for your marketing plan. Both first-time authors and those with existing "platforms" will benefit from the use of a series of events to systematically spread the word about your book release.

What is an author platform? Today's highly sought-after authors who receive sizeable advances on royalties from traditional publishers have built an audience who is hungry for their writing, which is what people in the book industry call an author platform. Examples of author platforms include activities such as hosting a radio show, syndicating articles, hosting a popular podcast show, social media followings or robust speaking schedules.

But it doesn't have to be difficult to build your author platform, with one little-known piece of knowledge. Media outlets such as TV stations, radio, newspapers and magazines are hungry for interesting people to interview. Every morning, producers of daily programming are seeking interesting people to interview with unique perspectives. As an author, you are the *very person* these media outlets are hungry to find.

Here is another way to think about a book from a broader perspective. Did you know that books are considered a "media outlet" by some experts? So if your book is a breakaway best seller and you sell 1 million copies, your media platform will have successfully reached .3% of the US population. Knowing this, however, most large publishers will consider a book as a "win" if it sells 10,000 copies.

The biggest question for you today is this: how do you become findable and sell a minimum of 10,000 copies? Many best-selling books will sell about 35,000 copies in a year. Better yet, what can we do to make your book so popular that it sells 1 million copies?

By following the series of steps in the coming pages, you and your story can be the center of attention. So, let's get started on your best-seller success story!

Book Marketing

The Achilles Heel of Authors

HE was in his 50's, and his steel-blue eyes could bore a hole through a sheet of steel.

"What do you mean I need to fund a $25,000 marketing campaign to create a best-selling book?" Rod's voice was steady, from years of practice leading teams for technology companies.

"Listen, Bryan; I didn't sign up for this—press releases, blog posts, kowtowing on social media, butt kissing on talk radio, writing jacket blurbs. I'm not a marketer. The only thing I'm going to write is my story, and my ideas will sell themselves."

I sighed, as I'd heard this story many times from authors across the globe. "I'm sure you can see that the work needs to be promoted," I offered, thumbing the corner of his thick manuscript. The meeting had dragged on longer than I'd expected, and as I glanced at my watch, I noticed that the chic seafood restaurant was now empty of lunchtime traffic.

"You're a promoter, and that's what I'm evaluating you for, isn't it?" he quipped.

"Um, actually I'm a publisher," I retorted. "You see, my job is to move books through distribution channels in order to exponentially expose readers to your writing. "

"Fine. Whatever. You can do that too. I'm just not going to do anything but write my stories. I've been leading teams for 20 years, and I'm not going to change that now." He took a sip of his iced tea. "I'll leave the marketing up to you to figure out. My game is technology and leadership."

The man was formidable. If it weren't for the fact that he was referred by a high-profile friend, I would have called for the check and gone to my next meeting.

No, book marketing was definitely not his thing. While he went on with a voice of authority, I mused about how he would come across at a book signing event.

But there was something about Rod that made me stay... Maybe it was the quality of his work; it really was good.

"I'll see what I can do."

Of Jangled Nerves and Disruption

I'm telling you about Rod because his situation is common among writers. Doing the daily work of a publisher, it is typical to deal with two types of authors: those whose motto is "I breathe; therefore I speak," and those whose motto is "I write; therefore I don't need to speak." One is outgoing; the other is not. One is people-oriented; the other is well qualified to work in a Forest Service fire watch tower—alone.

In both cases, their medium is words. And in both cases, "sale" is a four-letter word. Sales and marketing are the last things either of them wants to think about. They just want to work with the words they love.

In today's publishing environment, a love for words just isn't enough to get a finished book into the hands of readers. In fact, as I've said so often before, writing your book is only 10% of the work involved.

Unfortunately for authors like Rod, writing is all they know. The good news is that book publishers' team of people handle the tasks of editing, book design, sales and distribution. So many self-published authors try to take on all of these tasks at once and succeed at only a few—if any. It's just too much for one person to master.

New authors are a little less buffeted by the disruptive storms of change and technology than those who are more seasoned. But, anyone trying to keep up with a rapidly changing marketplace, like book publishing, has a case of jangled nerves. The average book launched will only go on to sell 500 copies (statistically), which is far below the expectations of people like Rod.

Selling the Sizzle

When structuring a marketing plan, one of the first questions to ask is, "Who is the audience for this book?" Your job is to seek out a segment of people who are hungry for your solutions or stories. It starts with assessing the playing field and crafting a story that resonates with a ready audience, ideally one that is accessible. How this story gets told is up to each author.

Here are a few examples of successful book marketing practices to get you started:

1. Blog tours: provide articles to high traffic bloggers

2. Radio shows: guest appearances on local or national radio shows

3. TV appearances: many New York Times best-selling authors get their start with appearances on Good Morning America

4. Social media: this is a great vehicle to build a big audience at a low cost

5. Bookstore signings: bookstores and libraries are great places to talk about your book

6. Speaking engagements: there is nothing more effective than sharing your ideas with a crowd to generate book orders

7. Advertising: it has never been easier than today to purchase advertising to a highly specific audience

8. Partnerships: professionals in this business build relationship with others who have large audiences, effectively structuring deals with the philosophy, "I'll scratch your back if you scratch mine."

What is noble about writing is putting ideas into the hands of readers around the world— readers who wouldn't have access to these ideas without easy access to a book.

Whether it's through libraries in Liberty, Kansas or on Kindles in the Amazon jungle, authors today have a reach that wouldn't have been possible otherwise. It's great to see them realize their goals.

For authors like Rod, a publishing relationship is a godsend. Now his business philosophies can be enjoyed everywhere, and his book sales show it. That's something any author can sink their teeth into.

The Book Launch Formula – Becoming a Hometown Hero

Have you ever noticed that no matter how successful you become, there's always someone who likes to knock you down a peg? Maybe it's an older sibling, an in-law or a friend from your high school days.

Maybe you are the exception, and you don't have anyone who fits this description. But I imagine if you think hard enough, the odds are high that you'll think of someone like this who is not too far from your inner circle.

The reason I bring it up is that, when it comes to your success as an author, this paradigm is repeated on a large scale in your hometown. The people who know you best, or for the longest time, are the ones who are least likely to give you the kudos you need to succeed on a grand scale.

There's always going to be a clique in your neighborhood who believe they know you too well. They figure you're a known quantity, and that there's little mystery to be revealed where you're concerned. These people don't mean to be dismissive or disrespectful. It's just human nature. It's only when you've got your name in lights within someone else's town that your neighbors will accept you as a success.

This means when it comes to your career, your hometown is the absolute best place to hone the skills it takes to successfully promote your book. It's nice and safe. No matter what you do, the people close to home are going to love you anyway and hold to their stubborn opinions. This makes it an excellent place to take risks, refine your media publicity skills and do lots of live events.

Book signings, media interviews and keynote addresses are the recipe for becoming a hometown hero. As your skills get more refined, you can get your act together and take it on the road. That's when your career will be ripe for that "overnight sensation" miracle we all read about in Huffington Post.

The Magic of Book Launch Events

If you're an author, it's essential to plan a series of promotional events in your local market to launch your book. Don't just release your book and try to convince people to buy it. Create tension and excitement in advance, centered around the big day your book will finally be available.

Think about it. How many sunny days have you spent with your nose pressed against the window, tapping on your keyboard instead of playing volleyball on the beach? How many family gatherings have you attended where people have asked, "How's your book coming along?" For that matter, how many events and celebrations have you missed because your writing came first?

There needs to be a payoff for the monumental investment of time, heart and soul that you've poured into your manuscript. Your fans and would-be followers want to share in the success of your book launch—which is why it needs to be a book launch instead of a book release.

Along with this launch comes the responsibility of having a series of appearances right in your hometown. It's not all that difficult to schedule these events. Just call your local bookstore and ask. The worst odds you face are 50/50. It's surprisingly easy to get your foot in the door, and many bookstore managers are hungry for authors to show up and create some buzz for their store.

In fact, Barnes & Noble stores have a position in each store called the "CRM" whose responsibility includes scheduling author signing events. So, ask for the "CRM" when requesting a signing in your local B&N store.

Libraries, schools, country clubs, civic organizations and social fraternities also make great venues for book signings. Usually, all it takes to schedule an event is making that initial phone call, then following the thread until your date is inked on the calendar.

Let the Local Media Be Your Mouthpiece

Once you schedule your book launch event, you'll want to make sure you invite colleagues, friends and family. But don't neglect the local media. This is a huge piece of the puzzle, yet so often it's overlooked by humble authors with a "Who? Me?" attitude. This is true even of retired corporate executives, professional speakers and others who've enjoyed success but are still tentative about promoting themselves in the author space.

Yes—the fact that you're having a book signing is a big event. Let the community share in your excitement. Put yourself out there, and you'll be amazed by the return you get on your investment of time and heart.

Contact local media outlets such as radio, TV and publishers. Journalists are receptive to submissions, and many strongly support the work of local authors. Also, don't be shy about reaching out to the media in neighboring cities as well. The farther afield you travel, the more likely you are to broaden the scope of your celebrity.

Local media coverage is not always easy to get, but it can be had for the right price. Often that price is simply your respect for their format. Look into the specific requirements of each of your local media outlets before you get in touch with them. You'll find that they're much the same across the board—with a few subtle variations on the theme. Make it easy for them to promote you, save them time, be interesting and be easy to reach.

A friend of mine got his product featured in the USA Today by counting the average number of words per article by the journalist who covers his topic. When he submitted his article, it took the journalist very little time to modify the article for publication to her tastes.

Working with the media is where having a press kit comes in handy.

When you have your author bio, book descriptions and press release prepared ahead of time, contacting the media is a breeze. And when you play by their format rules, you're handing them every reason to cover your book launch events.

Combining book launch events with local media promotion is a great recipe for becoming a hometown hero—one that plants the seeds of red carpet celebrity and stellar book sales. I've seen this happen many times in my career as a publisher and look forward to reading about your success stories.

2

The Art of Branding
for Authors

NOW that it is understood how to get discovered by the media, and how to structure your book launch sequence of events, it is time to consider how you are perceived by the public. The goal is to carve out a clear piece of "real estate" in the minds of the public, so when they hear your name, they know exactly what you represent.

The classic method of achieving this impression in the minds of the public is what marketers call Branding. In my career working with Fortune 500 companies, a team of people would spend close to a year conceptualizing a brand, designing it and rolling it out to the public. Authors often do not have the luxury of this kind of time, staff or the investment typically spent by big companies.

But, there is hope. Countless authors have clearly established their brand in the marketplace. How do they do it? This chapter distills the complexity of branding methodology into a process that you can implement without a team of experts in the art of branding.

So, let's explore how to craft your brand message and set a plan to make your message stick.

Your WHY – The Essence of a Personal Brand

"**WHY** do you do what you do?" This question comes to you from the young man sitting next to you on a recent flight. Like yours, his seat back is comfortably angled 30 degrees back, and his tray table is in the down position. You've both settled in.

The two of you are on a first-class flight home from Dubai. Fate and a travel agent have thrown you together, and now you're making chit-chat over strong coffee, colloquially known as Turkish coffee. It tastes good, and the caffeine/cardamom combo cuts through the morning fog of your mind. Last night's dinner-and-drinks with your client quickly turned into dessert-and-one-too-many.

"I mean," your seatmate continues, "what drives you to keep giving these keynote speeches?"

You've already swapped stories about the Zig Ziglar audios which you were surprised to learn were on his smartphone. His stories of singing Sinatra standards from a tiny stage where he gigged aboard a 120' private yacht last week seem to have gone dry for the moment, along with the cucumber water in your glass. Still, the young singer seems bent on keeping the conversation going.

"It sounds like you could just retire right now," he says, "and you wouldn't have to put up with these long flights and grueling schedules. Is it really worth it to be a keynote speaker? I mean, why do you keep doing it?"

"Why indeed…" you parrot, adjusting your glasses with a thick hand. "Dubai to LA seems like a long haul this morning, I can tell you that," you chuckle. "And I've got more of the same waiting for me at LAX—same hoopla, same glad-handing and photo ops. You know, I haven't thought about that question in a long time."

But his question is a good one, and you feel its heft in your mind like a gold ingot in the center of your palm—rare and worthy.

Your thoughts trail back a couple of days, back to the night you arrived in Dubai and the limo picked you up at the airport. Your client, the CEO, was already in the back seat, eager to be seen with you, arriving together at an exclusive gala at a towering hotel behind a velvet rope. The cameras and the crowds offered a heady glow of success.

That night was capped with too few hours of sleep in your suite on the concierge level, fruit and flowers in every room, scenting the air with their heavy perfume. You found a gift from the meeting planner thoughtfully left on the entry table—a silver monogrammed business card holder and a note of thanks. It was a nice touch, if a little impersonal. Back home, there was a closet in your office that was full of things like this—chachkies and souvenirs, corporate gifts from exotic ports of call where hoards had been swayed by the words you spoke.

But that's not the reason. Why then?

Your mind drifts back to your early career when you stood on the platform in a meeting hall at a local winery for 30 minutes; the audience mesmerized while you shared your best stuff. That talk was the springboard for the words you said in Dubai yesterday, and it launched a thousand opportunities for you. The warm feeling in your heart of touching the hundreds of people in that winery hall—influencing their lives—was as sweet as wine itself. You would have done it for free, but the back-of-room sales you made after the talk were a nice bonus. A whole new world had opened up for you that day.

Now you search your memory for an even deeper answer, and a vague form takes shape. You were meeting with a publisher over a cocktail, who was an old colleague who'd worked with you on that start-up years ago. The experience is like a private joke you share between the two of you, like veterans of war.

"Say, I'm writing a book," you told him casually, pulse racing. "Do you think you could give me some tips on how to make it successful...?"

Now the memory starts to flood back. You remember that you had been sweating this meeting for days, thinking your friend's professional advice would kill your enthusiasm, afraid he would laugh at your naiveté or tell you that your ideas were too controversial. You feared that the unique and precious thing inside you—the song that only you could write—would be silenced before anyone heard it. You were afraid that taking a chance, confiding in your friend, meant that your dream must live or die at that moment. You were afraid of terminal rejection, afraid that you would depart this earth with your music still inside you, afraid to let go of that burning fire in your heart.

You were afraid.

You couldn't bear the thought that your passion for these concepts was yours alone. You had to get the word out. It was your mission. You simply must tell others, because you knew that they could be changed if only they knew about the key that you had discovered for yourself. You knew that their lives would be better, easier and more provident if you could just reach them—if you could share the gems that you had come by through years of trial and error, of love and blood and sweat. You could shorten their learning curve, and you could help others by making their lives easier. You could change a piece of their world if you could just reach them with the message in your book.

And then it happened, the thing you couldn't have expected, though you'd dreamt of it often enough—your friend said yes.

"Sure," he smiled, "I'll help you publish it too, if you'd like. You might want to think about writing a talk to go along with that manuscript of yours. These things work best in tandem."

Now the memory fades as the flight attendant brushes past you, gliding down the aisle. The young man in the seat next to you sweeps the shock of hair from his eyes and searches your face. The hum of the jet drones on, like a bass note in the dance of your life. "Why wouldn't you want to put down roots, or retire early and get off this merry-go-round?" the young man says. "I mean, what makes you want to trek the planet and say the things you do?"

In the back of your mind, you hear a Ziglar quote which comes back to your mind like a distant memory, "You will get everything in life you want, if you will just help enough other people get what they want."

And suddenly, in a flash, you connect with your reason why, that driving force that silently compels you to push forward... serving others.

The Rule of 7

It's funny how you can be talking to someone, and they seem to understand what you're saying. They smile and nod; even interject a comment here or there.

But are they really getting you? Once the conversation is over, it's like it never happened.

Maybe a few days later the subject comes up again. You hash it out one more time, and this time it seems like you're getting through.

But no. It's not that they're obstinate. It's just that any new idea requires repeated exposure to become internalized. That is how the brain works.

Studies show that people need to hear an idea seven times before it sinks in.

Think about that the next time you ask your teenager to take out the garbage. You don't have to hound them until you're "blue in the face." Just tighten up your repetitions, and you'll compress the amount of time it takes to drive your point home. After a while, it becomes automatic, and you don't have to mention it again. Well… maybe a couple more times.

This brings us to the all-important topic of exposures in marketing campaigns, and what I call the *Rule of Seven*. When you can leverage this rule, the seven exposures get your audience to "see the light" and make a purchase.

It sounds simple—and it is—but it's not without technique. Let's cover a few simple rules that you can apply to your book or new product launch to drive sales and create evangelists.

Sales Lessons from the Marketing World

Did you ever notice product displays when you go to a retail store or mall? The brand jumps out at you every time you walk by.

By your third pass, you stop and notice that the featured widget might actually be something you could use to solve a problem or engage a desire. In fact, the product could be tremendously effective. It might even change your life. But the first time you passed by, it didn't even register.

During my Fortune 500 marketing career, I was responsible for rolling-out a retail kiosk for a brand-new kind of service. It was a revolutionary product, and our Marketing team had a pretty robust ad budget to support the US launch. Amazingly enough, our Sales team was successful in putting this display in 20,000 retail locations across North America. Failure was not an option.

You would think that with all those locations and gobs of money for advertising, all we had to do was wait for the checks to come rolling in. But the fundamentals of consumer awareness apply across the board. We used the *Rule of Seven* to drive messaging home and make sales.

Using the One-To-Many Approach... Seven Times!

When you are planning your next social media effort or ad campaign, there are a few principles to consider. You can use them when deciding how many ad exposures it will take to reach your audience effectively. It still takes seven repetitions to generate awareness of a brand, a book or service, but you can do it much more efficiently.

In our campaign to drive sales in those 20,000 retail locations, we focused on messaging that went from one-to-many. We carefully planned a series of messages reaching millions of "influencers," called Early Adopters. The Early Adopters in this industry embraced new ideas and technologies earlier than most, and we knew they would evangelize our product for us.

The structure of the marketing campaign for this product was built around the *Rule of Seven*. Here is how the campaign was structured to reach the magic number of exposures:

1. Trial coupons in Free Standing Inserts (FSI's) in leading newspapers

2. Direct mail campaign

3. Print flyers, delivered by a partner company

4. In-store advertising in grocery stores, where most people shop 2.3 times (on average) each week

5. Television commercials

6. On-kiosk advertising in major retail locations such as WalMart, Target, and Costco

7. Sponsorship at a series of sporting events

Each one of these venues invited multiple exposures and drove home the message to generate awareness, familiarity and ultimately, trial. This marketing philosophy can be applied and works for new product launches, and can even be effective for a book launch campaign.

As you plan your next marketing campaign, remember the Rule of Seven. How can you plan your book launch campaign to leverage the Rule of Seven used by professional marketing teams?

Here is a sample idea of how to create 7 repetitions of the message around your book that does not require the multi-million dollar budgets of professional marketers.

1. Plan a daily series of social media posts. If you can schedule 3-months of daily posts, you will earn top marks in your class!

2. Send regularly scheduled emails.

3. Schedule a series of speaking events.

4. Hand-out bookmarks promoting your book at live events.

5. Clearly establish the profile of your target readers, and reach them via an advertising campaign online (Google ads, Facebook ads, Amazon ads, etc.).

6. Schedule bookstore signing tour.

7. Ask the local media for a radio or TV appearance.

Your patience in generating seven repetitions will prove that 7 just might be your lucky number!

Branding for the Big Bucks

Where could your business, your speaking business or book sales go if you released all your limitations? With the right company brand or personal brand behind your business endeavors, you can break through untold barriers and realize your professional dreams.

What exactly is branding? Your branding is the way people perceive you and your mission—whether it's your company, your personal career branding at work or even your private objectives. Branding distills your ideology into a series of elements that together create the look-and-feel of an ideal.

Branding is the practice of using your business name, logo, slogans, color choices and other assets in your marketing communications so that consumers can easily recognize you. In short, it's your image.

Your brand communicates the qualities, ideas, emotions (if you're good) and user experience that your products present to the marketplace. Using these assets in all of your business communications will reinforce your brand with every consumer touch.

The largest and most successful companies in the world all use these strategies to build their brand equity into billions of dollars. The industry giants of yesterday and today—Google, Apple, Tide, Microsoft, Coca-Cola, Xerox, Kodak, Nike, Ford, Disney, Kellogg's, and many more—all successfully built their brand to household name recognition. Having worked professionally with 6 of these mega-brands personally, there are things we can learn from these best of class brands.

Consumers know these brands by heart and trust the products enough to purchase them without debate. The safety, quality and dependability of the product is assumed—even expected.

Of Rutted Roads and Grizzly Bears

My career began working for one of these mega-brands—Kodak—and it literally changed the way I perceive my place in the world. At the time, the Kodak brand was the 4th most valuable brand in the world, with a value on the balance sheet in the billions of dollars. This brand association also has had a deep and lasting effect on my career success. By associating with a major household name, my employers, clients and colleagues look at me a little differently. Some of the brand's magic dust brushed off on me, and it influenced the success in my early business career.

Early in my career, I landed one of the largest Sales territories a young guy in Sales could hope for. It was also in one of the most remote areas on the planet. My job was to sell Kodak film throughout the State of Alaska. It may sound prestigious to have a territory that is a third of the land mass of the United States, but before you get overly impressed, I'd like to put this data point into perspective.

Alaska is not an easy place to promote a brand. First, there are more bears in Alaska than people. Second, half the state's population lives in one city, Anchorage, and Alaska is the largest State in the USA—in fact, the State is one-third the size of what Alaskans call the "Lower 48." You just can't drive across it in a day. In fact, most parts of the state are undrivable. One of the most popular modes of transportation is the float plane. Even these hardy vehicles have trouble reaching vast expanses in the rugged wilderness, largely because there's just nowhere to land.

Let me put it this way: As a Kodak man, I had a lot of muddy ground to cover in my shiny loafers, and my wide yellow tie was a little hard to miss among the fireweed on the tundra. Even the herds of caribou would roll their eyes when they saw me coming.

I'll never forget the time when a sales call took me to a gold mine located some half a day's drive from the big city where I lived. I thought someone at the home office had made a typo on my sales sheet—either that or they were playing a practical joke. I mean, who sells Kodak film in Hope, Alaska? I couldn't image a gold mine wanting anything to do with my goods.

The road to the mine was a dirt track, now awash in runoff from the spring breakup. The farther away I got from the main highway, the more I was sure there'd been some kind of mistake as my Chevy Celebrity bounced through the potholes.

It was more than 15 rutted miles after I left the pavement before I saw another soul. You can imagine my relief when I turned a corner to find this replica of an old western town—a fly-in tourist attraction, a relic from the days of the Klondike catering to Japanese tourists who wanted a wilderness experience. I wandered into the only open building I could find, a tavern populated with a few old salts that smelled of smoke, bacon and Jack Daniels.

Yet even in the farthest, most remote corners of the world, the Kodak brand was recognized, and I was welcomed to pull-up a stump at the table for a hot cup of coffee in a tin cup. After talking to the bearded mountain man at the end of the table, it seemed that tourists to this gold panning paradise preferred Kodak film over Fuji film... all I had to do was show up and write the order.

Branding does more than creating recognition. It builds trust and loyalty among the consumers in your market, allowing you to penetrate future markets with new product offerings more successfully—no matter how remote they are. Successful branding carries awareness and trust, even in a land populated with more bears than people.

So, as you think through the marketing efforts for your book or speaking business, pay attention to your brand. You'll discover many unintended benefits by crafting a message that will stick in the minds of your audience.

3

How to Get Quality Book Endorsements from Celebrities

IN the realm of book marketing, there's an axiom that goes like this:

"If I say it, it's up for debate; if someone else says it, it must be true."

Third-party validation is a sure-fire method of getting people to draw a conclusion about you or your book. In fact, a well-known endorser has proven to add instant credibility to books and professional speakers.

Do you doubt this? You can prove it for yourself—try this exercise. Decide for yourself which of these statements sounds better if you say it, or if it sounds best coming from a trusted third-party expert:

- This book is the most efficient, effective path to living up to the potential inside you.

- No other author delivers so much yet still leaves the reader hungry for more.

- Each delicious word lolls around on the palette like a chocolate-kissed gem—you'll want to try these foolproof recipes for yourself.

- The author is clearly the most knowledgeable person of our time and a credit to society.

- Put on your thinking cap—this book is lightning in a bottle. You won't be able to put it down.

Got your answers? Good.

It probably didn't take you long to decide that if you had written these blurbs about yourself, you would have stopped at #2 (if you were feeling generous).

But if any of these quotes about your work came from a head of State, a New York Times best-selling author or the winner of a Nobel Prize, you'd probably crack the cover on your book and read at least a couple of lines. (Chocolate-kissed gems, anyone?)

Third-party validation is the most compelling reason to go after book endorsements for your work. It's also a very intimidating step on the list of things that an author must do to get noticed in the crowded book marketplace. In terms of phobias, requesting endorsements is not far behind root canals, furry South American spiders and that dreaded Numero Uno… public speaking!

But unlike the items in the paragraph above, getting book endorsements doesn't have to be all that scary. There's really very little risk involved, and the benefits far outweigh the price of your request. The few steps below will help you ask for—and get—the endorsements that are so critical to your book's success.

It's simple. Don't ask, don't get.

Ask, and you just might collect a priceless recommendation from someone you really admire. Having the thought leader in your field say good things about you is sure to up your ratings, not to mention your book sales. So, ask for the endorsement.

Five Essentials for Getting Quality Book Endorsements

Now that we've established this is an important step to take, let's take a look at what you need to do to get your first Yes.

1. **Ask an Author** - Authors are usually responsive to requests for book endorsements. They "get" it, so start with the experts in your field or genre. You'd be surprised how easy it is to get a response, especially when you remind them of the exposure they will gain from your marketing.

2. **Ask an Expert** - Experts also thrive on exposure and professional courtesy. Aim high when asking for an endorsement. Using these tips, you can expect a 20-50% response rate using this system.

3. **Send Your Endorsement Letter** - Starting with a letter, request an endorsement for your book. Your letter can either be inserted into the body of an email, or it can be mailed as a physical letter. Your tone should be complimentary without sucking up, and you'll need to briefly state something that the two of you have in common. Make sure they know how to contact you in reply.

   A while ago I sent an endorsement request to a famous author whose book has sold 25 million copies. His book was also released as a major motion picture, complete with mega-stars playing the leading roles. He sent me a response saying "maybe," based on his ability to squeeze-in this request during his upcoming new release book tour and red carpet movie premiere schedule.

4. **Send Your Book Review Materials** - Once your endorsement prospect has answered your letter and said, "Yes, or, Maybe," it's time to give them the tools to do the job. Offer an at-a-glance summary of your book, the Introduction, the Table of Contents, and a couple of sample chapters. Use your judgment about whether to mail a copy of your materials or send it via email. If you send an email, provide a website link with a protected URL where the endorser can download a PDF as some folks are shy about opening email attachments they receive from strangers.

5. **Include Endorsement Samples** - Make some suggestions about what your endorser might say. Prepare three or four sample endorsements, since people in your network may ask you to write the

endorsement for them. Make the comments easy to digest, but also let them glow a little around the edges.

To Best Seller Status and Beyond

The endorsements you collect can be quite valuable for you and your book, long beyond launch day. It helps to think of the time and effort involved as an investment. What you put in will return to you in the form of dividends.

Book endorsements will be featured on your website, Amazon.com, in your marketing materials, on your book jacket, on sell sheets that are sent to retail book buyers and many other places.

The time and resources you invest in this stage of your marketing campaign are more than worth it. The right book endorsement will open doors for your writing endeavors, your book and your paid speaking opportunities.

4

Creating a Product Funnel:
The Business Side of Writing

ONCE your brand has been established, your thinking naturally starts to shift into what types of product offerings are most valuable to your audience. The approach in this chapter is geared to non-fiction authors, but the principles may apply to many types of books ranging from cookbooks to children's books.

Let's explore the business side of writing non-fiction books. For multi-million dollar earning authors, often their book is a component of their overall business strategy. An important part of the business strategy includes the various product offerings offered to the public.

In this section, we will explore ideas for product development coupled with the concept of a "Product Funnel." A product funnel is a series of products which sequentially lead your audience from one product to the next, with increasing profitability as people consume your series of products.

But where do you start?

The Product Funnel for Authors:
How to Build a Product Funnel

Building a product funnel is a fundamental item for your speaking and writing business. Yet few efforts are more misunderstood in the information business—from Internet Marketers to Professional Speakers—and creating the means to effectively sell products online or offline is largely a mystery.

Getting this right can be the difference between having a luncheon featuring beef bourguignon by the green at the Pig & Whistle or packing bologna on white bread in a brown paper bag.

So just what is a product funnel, and how do you use it? Is it some mechanical gadget that baristas use to whip up a mocha Frappuccino? Is it the end piece of a conveyor belt found in a state-of-the-art Amazon warehouse? Hardly. Let's start with a few basics.

A product funnel is the sequence of exposures or "touches" that your prospective customer goes through before deciding to buy from you. It begins with the initial touch and manages your prospect's buying relationship with you all the way through product upsells and special offers.

Whether you're using advertising, email marketing, social networks, live events or a combination of media, your customers learn your "music" through repetition—like a song on the radio. Typically, you find a set of marketing vehicles that works for you and repeat their use until your prospects absorb enough information to make buying decisions.

The magic number here is seven—that's how many exposures it takes to cross *The Trust Gap*. It takes seven exposures for a prospect to become a buyer, building trust and rapport with each contact.

You don't need to be a professional master buyer to bring home the sales. All it takes is a few simple efforts to get the job done. Once you set up your sales funnel and drive traffic to your products, they will practically sell themselves.

The Attraction Factor

Years ago, Pepsi made waves when the company opted not to advertise during the Superbowl, choosing instead to channel its mega ad budget into social media marketing. This was a stunning development in the world of advertising, and it heralded a new era. It meant that, for the moment, the playing field was level. It also meant the death of "salesy" sales tactics.

Pepsi didn't exactly create this new paradigm; it merely tapped into events already unfolding. The writing was on the wall. People no longer wanted to be sold to. They wanted sincere product recommendations from their friends, and they wanted to try before they buy. The era of the online review and the product giveaway was born.

Before this Superbowl change-up by a mega-brand, only savvy marketers were giving away a free report or eCourses to attract new subscribers to their mailing list. After Pepsi's landmark decision, this tactic became the new norm. Freemiums were no longer the fodder of Internet Marketing geeks who slaved away during the wee hours. The "freemium offer" was now mainstream.

Building the Perfect Blend

The Giveaway: The purpose of giving away something of value—such as a book chapter or an audio recording—is to build trust and rapport. As Dale Carnegie so aptly put it during the early part of the last century, people want to do business with those they know, like, and trust. Getting the giveaway item right takes skill and effort, and makes a material difference in your campaign. Give this aspect of your campaign some effort.

The List: Giving something away for free does not work without a list to tell people about your offer. Adding followers, names, and email addresses to your lists allows you to create multiple exposures to your efforts. If you are new to this business, then know that building an email list is the "gold standard" of lists. Social media lists can be more cost effective to build versus email… just remember that attention spans are micro-short.

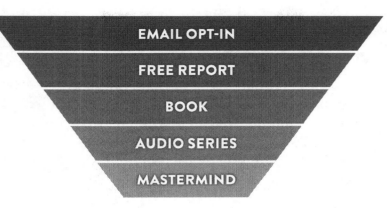

The Product: From the initial contact through repeated exposures, you can encourage your prospect to check out your well-crafted sales page for your entry-level product. Let's say you're offering a limited time discount on your book to celebrate its launch. You can mention this several times over the course of your email series and include a link to the product page, or what insiders call a "squeeze page." When brainstorming your product line, consider the top 10 product formats common to speakers and authors.

The Upsell: Once your prospect clicks through the link and opts to buy, you can offer them a second product to purchase while they are in the buying mood. This upsell tactic doesn't have to be limited to a single product. It could be a bundle of products, a set or system, a special coaching session, a webinar—even an upcoming conference.

The Follow Up: Once your prospect makes it to your list of customers, you can market to them in a whole new way. You can offer additional discounts, build excitement over new product launches, keep in touch with your latest endeavors, or otherwise leverage the attention of the audience you've built.

Using product upsells as part of your sales funnel is the surest way to double or triple your income from your marketing investment. Understanding your sales funnel as the key to your money-making endeavors can unlock the door to prosperity for you. Walking through that door is up to you.

Professional marketers will use various tools online to structure their product funnel, and there are hundreds to choose from. As you research what tools work for you, here are a couple to consider to kick-start your research:

- ClickFunnel

- Kajabi

- InfusionSoft

Top 10 Book Derivatives

As you are thinking about your product funnel, let's explore what product options are available to you as an author. As you review this list, write down how your writing can be multi-purposed into other profitable products.

Here is an overview of the top 10 types of product types which are popular for authors with multi-million dollar businesses. While this is not an exhaustive list, this list is designed to stimulate thinking about which product derivatives are right for your business.

1. **Book:** This is pretty obvious as you embark upon the journey to build your author platform. But consider the 3 main types of book derivatives, ranked by the percent of revenues received by each product derivative by North American authors: Physical books represent 65% of the revenue mix, eBooks represent 25% and unabridged audiobooks represent 10% of the revenue mix from your book.

2. **Audio programs:** Audio programs come in various configurations. Popular recorded audios include a 6- to 10-part series of 30-minute studio recordings. Other revenue opportunities exist in recording a keynote speech presentation and distributing it for sale.

3. **Subscription Service / Membership Program:** This product offering is increasingly popular with the professionals in the business of writing where a daily, weekly or monthly product is delivered. The product delivery can be electronic (such as online video, articles or audio recording), or the product can be physically mailed in the format of a book-of-the-month model.

4. **Webinars:** A webinar is an online audio or video program, which can be delivered live or be pre-recorded. The webinar offers valuable information coupled with audience interaction, which makes an outstanding learning environment.

5. **Tools or Templates:** Authors choose to offer valuable tools within their product funnel designed to help people within their industry. These tools could include this sampling of ideas: a daily prioritization system, templates (such as legal documents) or pre-built spreadsheets which help manage complex calculations.

6. **Coaching & Consulting:** Daily, weekly or monthly coaching offerings are quite popular, which can be delivered in a variety of ways. The coaching or consulting delivery can include face-to-face, phone meetings, social media private groups, video conferencing and more.

7. **Speaking Engagements:** For the author who loves the energy of a live crowd, public speaking offers a tremendous opportunity for authors. Some authors successfully book 60 speaking engagements per year, which represents a 7-digit revenue opportunity in this product derivative alone.

8. **Mastermind Programs:** Organizing live or virtual meetings on a periodic basis is a popular method for authors to obtain very profitable sources of income to support their business. There are tremendous synergies created when like-minded people meet to pursue their passions.

9. **Licensed Merchandise:** You can probably think of examples of merchandise that is created around the theme of a book. If you have established a following of passionate readers, then licensed merchandise is highly recommended. This can come in the form of journals, calendars, mugs and mouse pads. Taking this concept can be taken even further to include themed travel built around your ideas. I've seen authors take fans to Europe on themed cooking tours, themed cruises and more.

10. **Apps & Software:** Securing digital real estate on phones and screens is a valuable place to reinforce your brand image. Creating a custom mobile app is

an excellent tool for achieving this goal. Also, creating software that helps people perform complex tasks is another lucrative option as a derivative of your work.

5

How to Get Media Attention
with Public Relations

AT the heart of an effective book launch is the strategy for getting media attention. As a result of doing media appearances, not only are you generating mass awareness of your book but you are also organically driving people into bookstores who will be asking for your book. Imagine if your influence could spread all the way from Portland, Maine to Portland, Oregon.

So, how difficult is it to get media appearances? I mean, who can possibly get people across an entire country interested in a single book release? In this section, we will explore the sequential steps in getting media attention. The essential tools to build include a Media Kit and a Press Release.

These materials, coupled with a recipe for running your own media campaign, will get you started. Some authors choose to work with a professional Public Relations to do the work for you. Others will elect the do-it-yourself approach presented in this chapter. It's your choice which approach is right for you, for when public relations is done right, it is proven to create significant influence in the marketplace.

5 Tips to Getting National Media Attention

If you're an author or a Fortune 500 executive, you've got your work cut out for you in terms of besting the competition. The requirements to run a successful marketing campaign are fairly specific, and you've got to have an edge, or what I call a **superpower**. Many hugely successful authors have a superpower to success. When you find your superpower, it's like stomping down the pedal of a 12-cylinder twin turbo Mercedes.

It's a bit like the difference between playing a friendly game of tennis at the public courts of Coronado Island near San Diego, and playing at the $88M world-class tennis stadium in Indian Wells built by Oracle CEO Larry Ellison.

There's nothing wrong with the tennis courts at Coronado—they're wonderful. In fact, there's nothing like swinging a racket beneath the shade of an emperor palm harborside, watching yachts bob up and down as you serve, and heading to the Coronado Beach Resort around the corner to cool down with a cold beverage after your match.

In fact, on a sunny Tuesday morning in February there's little competition for a tennis court on Coronado Island. Just drive up, park curbside, and swing away in the fresh morning air. While the rest of the world is jockeying for position to order a latte at the espresso bar, there's little to compare with the feeling of breezing over the bridge to Coronado for a match before lunch.

But this is a very different scene from playing professional tennis, such as at the Indian Wells Tennis Gardens in Palm Springs. The competition to be on the court is all but insurmountable, reserved for those players who are the envy of amateurs. Those rare tennis players who make it to this level have an edge. They have found a superpower to success, such as hitting a rocket-like forehand down the line for a winner while running at a full sprint.

Just Like Superman

If you are releasing any product, from a book release to an incredibly cool mobile app, media skills must be honed to amplify your message. The moment you publish your work and begin to promote it, you are competing with big international money for the same spotlight.

In marketing, I cut my teeth working for three of the world's largest companies whose Brands were in the top 10 most valuable Brands in the world. After a few decades of this work, I decided to step out on my own and start an online advertising agency right in the heart of what is now called "the Roaring 90's." As the company was growing exponentially, we were suddenly offered a buyout by a big publically traded company New York. At the time, our marketing approach was working exclusively with a highly select clientele, and it allowed us to compete with much larger, less nimble opponents.

I remember one day leaning against the water cooler in the company headquarters in Manhattan on 29th & Broadway, complaining about the incredible competition we faced. The question was, how were we to compete on a national landscape with a measly $2 million launch budget when my big brand competitors were spending $100 million per year? I felt like Jack who climbed the magic beanstalk, only to find he had to slay a giant before he could go home to his wife and kids at 6:00.

As authors, very few have access to a $2 million budget for a book release. So how does an author amplify their message on a national or international stage without a 7-digit marketing budget?

The book industry is a very competitive industry. In non-fiction, there are hundreds of thousands of new releases annually (in North America). Large book superstores will stock 75,000 total titles each season, with a fraction of their shelf space dedicated to new non-fiction book titles.

With statistics like these, getting the word out and rising above the competition can seem nearly impossible. But, from a marketing perspective, authors have a hidden superpower. Very few authors take full advantage of this lack of parity, and that means it can amount to a backdoor to success for those who choose to hone their marketing prowess.

Winning the Big Match

Big media companies love to interview authors. If you are Lexus or Disney, you typically need to buy massive exposure from media companies to get the message out. Insightful authors can often obtain massive media exposure for pennies on the dollar, simply because of their status as a thought leader.

The trick to leveling the competitive playing field is to build your marketing tool belt. Here are 5 tips to create your superpower:

> **Tip 1:** Create an inventory of content to post on your blog and social media accounts. Take note of the unique guidelines required for writing copy appropriate for LinkedIn (short articles), Facebook (25-50 words with a meme or video), and Twitter (144 characters with strategic use of hashtags). Get in motion, and stay in motion, consistently pushing your message forward.

> **Tip 2:** Write a series of articles on your area of expertise that can be posted to article directories, submitted to magazines, and posted to LinkedIn as well. Make sure your content includes your best keyword research, and incorporate these keywords in everything you post.

> **Tip 3:** Social media posts and articles must always include images, so start collecting licensed images that are compelling and relate to your material. Try getting 10-20 images that are a good fit by doing keyword research on your area of expertise, whether it be making an awesome pie crust or agile software development.

Tip 4: Work with a publisher who has a sales team calling on bookstores. To maneuver around your competition, getting your book into bookstores requires sales calls on both chain buyers and people who coordinate bookstore signing events. Hundreds of thousands of new books are released each year, and a publisher's track record on producing winners makes a huge difference in getting retail shelf space on a national level. With ebook sales on the decline and new indie bookstores opening at a rapid clip, getting physical bookstore distribution is essential in today's climate for books.

Tip 5: Leverage your superpower as an author and get media appearances. This is the magic ingredient in penetrating national consciousness with your book. If you are able to break through in 3 markets in the US, your chances of success increase exponentially.

The question is, are you happy with the results you've achieved so far? Or are you ready to slip through the backdoor to success by leveraging your superpower as an author? The competition is keen, but the choice is yours. And the rewards are rich indeed!

Book Publicity Media Kits – The 5 Essential Elements Journalists Need

Successfully marketing your book basically means letting people know that it exists. After all, you wrote down your best ideas so that others would read and enjoy them. Getting more book sales translates to more people sharing your best ideas—fact or fiction—and benefitting from them.

As the person who's primarily responsible for promoting your book, one smart move you can make is to leverage the huge media potential available to authors. Doing this will mean you won't be the only person touting your book. You'll have massive media outlets helping you out.

The problem with using traditional publicity is that the process can be intimidating. Buyers for book distributors and retail bookstores decide how many copies to order per outlet based on publicity and demand. Getting regional or national exposure helps drive that demand. But how can you get publicity for your book when there's so much competition for face time in the media?

The answer lies in preparation. Having a complete media kit prepared ahead of time for all your publicity contacts will ensure that they have access to everything they need to decide to put you in front of their audience. In fact, a media kit will stack the odds in your favor, and getting mass exposure becomes a matter of making yourself available to media outlets.

Time-starved magazine editors, radio personalities and TV talk show hosts are all looking for a comprehensive and professional presentation. They need to see a total package that will help them out with their stories. If you can present them with the material they need ahead of time, you are much more likely to land that interview, book review or feature. This preparation comes in the form of the media kit.

The 5 Essentials of a Book Media Kit

There is a wide assortment of materials that authors include in their media kit, but many of them are overkill for a journalist in a hurry. Sometimes less really is more. Your complete media kit should include the following elements:

1. **Your Author Biographies**

   Yes, you need more than one bio. Depending on the length, these may include your professional background, your experience as an author, and even information about your lifestyle such as where you live.

   Your bios should be offered in the following lengths:

   - 2 lines (120 characters)

   - Short bio (50 words)

   - Medium bio (100 words)

   - Long bio (400 to 600 words)

2. **Your Press Release**

   This should include meaty, useful content, citing you as an authority on the topic with a reference to your book. It should not be an announcement that you've written a book. There's no quicker way to bore a journalist, and these are the people you want to excite.

   Besides meaty content and sound bites, your press release should include the following often omitted data:

   - Headline up to 20 words

- Subheading (optional

- Dateline (City, State, Date)

- Call to action at the bottom of the release

- Your contact information—don't make people work hard to find you

3. **A Book Synopsis and Sample Chapter**

   Pull your most important information onto one sheet. Include a cover image, the title and sub-title, table of contents and key selling points. Include Reviews and Endorsements if you have them. If you don't have them, then set aside time to get them. Include book review excerpts if you have them, such as "This book is a thrill ride! I couldn't put it down."

4. **Publicity Photos**

   Offer more than one type of publicity photo. Make sure these images are professionally done with nicely balanced contrast and clear, sharp focus.

   - Image of your book cover created by a professional book graphic designer

   - Head shot of just you with even lighting and an approachable facial expression

   - A candid shot of you in a relevant context, showing you in an environment that relates to your topic

5. **Sample Interview Questions, Tips, Quotes and Sound Bites**

   People in the media may not have the time to read your book, so make it easy for them to understand your work. Include sample interview questions in your media kit. Radio and TV personalities especially love these. Journalists love to see list of tips that they can reprint in connection with your book. All media people love to use quotes and sound bites, so feed them what they want.

The thing to remember about your media kit is that it's a work in progress. It will constantly need to be updated. If you set it and forget it, in time, it will forget you. Stay active in the life of your book's publicity. With proper care and feeding, and it will provide you with fat royalty checks for a long time to come.

How to Write a Press Release for a Book Launch

For authors seeking that elusive Best Seller status, self-promotion can be your best tool for driving laser sharp traffic and increasing book sales.

Of all the self-promotion options available, distributing press releases is probably the most overlooked method. It's unfortunate because it can be highly effective—especially if your press release is picked up by a major news outlet, journal or magazine. In a few rare cases, it can even launch you to stardom.

The mistake most authors make with this tactic is believing that the launch of their book is news in itself. Nothing could be more boring to the buying public than banging your drum about launch dates and press runs.

Your angle needs to be one that touts your problem and solution, mentions you as an author or expert, and includes the name of your book almost as an incidental point of fact.

The topic of your press release needs to be timely or even cheeky—something with an off-beat hook that captures the reader's imagination. You've got to make them feel what you feel about your topic, then demonstrate that reading your book is the only logical next step.

Besides being a gripping read, a good press release is timely, newsworthy, and contains links to your book listing so readers can get more information about it. Every day, publishers, editors and journalists pick up press releases as they mine for breaking news within an industry. This offers valuable exposure for you and your book.

One success story to share is from professional speaker Keith Harrell, who had an extraordinary experience with this kind of publicity. One day Keith was contacted by a reporter who had seen his press release. The reporter was writing a "Day in the Life" story about half a dozen professional speakers for a financial newspaper.

Sounds a little drab, doesn't it? I mean, who wants to be relegated to a by-the-way blurb in a dry-as-toast financial journal like this? That's what all the other speakers thought. In fact, the reporter had contacted six speakers and asked each one for an interview. But Keith was the only one who responded to her call, so the reporter ran a full-page article devoted just to Keith. Lucky Keith!

It turned out that the reporter was writing this article for the Wall Street Journal—yes, THAT dry-as-toast little financial journal. Through this one event, Keith Harrell went from virtual obscurity to fame overnight. This led to his success with a New York Times best-selling book and a multi-million dollar speaking business.

I have to add that in order for the reporter to contact Keith in the first place, Keith's press release needed to contain certain elements, and it had to be a good read. It had to capture the reporter's imagination, and it needed a clear call to action at the end. Here's an outline you can use for your own press releases.

First, plan to write more than one. Then, make sure that your press releases all contain the necessary elements, which I've listed below. Make it easy for anyone interested in your work to find you, contact you and promote you. Finally, distribute your press releases to as many relevant media hubs as possible.

In your press release, include links back to your website to drive more traffic and create buzz about your website. Writing articles and distributing them via partner websites and article distribution websites (such as ezinearticles.com) are also excellent sources of free traffic.

Contents of a Standard Press Release

- Headline - This can be up to 20 words
- Subhead - This is optional

○ Dateline - City, State, Date of press release

○ Article beginning - Catch the reader's attention, including a problem and solution

○ Author quote - this a meaty and compelling sound byte

○ Author info - A paragraph or two about the author

○ Book info - A paragraph or two about the book about the book

○ Contact - Include links for review copies and media interviews with you, as well as your website address

○ CTA - Conclude with a clear, compelling Call To Action

○ Hashtags - Include social media hashtags

○ About the Author - your author biography, about 500 words

For Non-Fiction: Lead your press release with the main problem and its solution in the first paragraph. What problem does your book solve? What solution will readers find? Lead the press release audience to your book obliquely. That is, state the problem and solution, then mention that your book supports this premise. Include anywhere from 3 to 7 tips from your book, and tell people how they can find out more. In an ideal world, tie-in your press release with current news for the best chance of getting picked up by major news outlets.

For Fiction: Lead with the key character at the beginning of the press release. Include the emotional angle of your premise. Tell people what emotions they will experience as they read the book, and help them preview their reading experience. As you write your press release, be clear about your target audience, and speak directly to them. Then, follow the recent news and see if there is an angle to tie-in your book or topic into breaking news.

Write your press releases for consumers, bloggers, journalists and the Google search algorithm. There are several large news services where you can distribute press releases with newsworthy information to reporters worldwide. Some of these include PRNewsWire.com and businesswire.com, to name just a couple.

As you dive into this promotional medium, you'll find a whole new world to discover. Now... get cracking! The world is waiting to discover you.

Planning a Do-It-Yourself (DIY) Media Tour

As a speaker or an author on the way to publishing your next book, the time to plan your public relations (or PR) strategy is upon you. You'll hear literary agents and publishers talking about your "platform." Let's explore the essentials of getting your platform built.

Authors have two essential choices to generate buzz from coast to coast on an affordable budget: 1) Hire a PR firm to do the work for you, which can get pricey, or 2) Plan and run your own PR campaign. Today, let's focus on the latter using DIY steps to build the platform for your book launch.

The game plan for a book launch sets the stage for the payoff in book sales and reputation. As an author, you've made a monumental investment of time, heart and soul into your manuscript.

Realistically, it takes about three to six months to build excitement and demand in the marketplace for your book. First comes the need to create interest, tension and excitement centered around your book's core message.

Where many book launches have enjoyed multi-million dollar budgets, not many authors have these kinds of resources to launch their book. You'd be surprised at how accessible the strategy is for typical authors, if you follow the same steps as the big budget pros in this business.

Getting Madison Avenue Results on a Main Street Budget

Two of my favorite PR recommendations have no cost associated with them at all. These favored do-it-yourself PR tactics are Blog Tours and Podcasting. These methods are so powerful that PR firms use them consistently with exceptional results. Many authors find these PR strategies accessible to the average person and choose to do the work themselves.

Podcast Tour: Podcasting is on the rise with well over 57 million active listeners in 2016. 21% of Americans have listened to a podcast episode recently (to compare, 21% of Americans are on Twitter and 13% use Spotify). It can be an effective tool for attracting attention to your book. With a podcast, people all over the world can access the ideas you talk about and create a more personal relationship with you.

I've seen authors build up a massive following using podcasts that highlight excerpts of their books or existing audio recordings. There's something enticing about a book either read by the author, a discussion around your topic or an excerpt from a keynote speech. No one else can offer such shades of nuance.

It's possible to get thousands of faithful fans this way—fans who will become aware of your book. These fans are quite valuable because not only will they buy your book, but they may become loyal customers who purchase your audio series, coaching or consulting services.

The powerhouse of podcast traffic is Apple's iTunes. However, there are other venues available to host your podcasts such as Stitcher and other podcatcher sites offering a dedicated following with little investment from you except your time.

It may take a little while to build up your following, but once you do, you will be amazed at the response.

Also, another effective podcast strategy is to set up your own podcast show.

Blog Promotion: Doing a Blog Tour is a cost-effective way to get exposure for your ideas. In aggregate, Bloggers have a huge center of influence. Getting your ideas and articles into these centers of influence can be a highly credible method for getting book exposure. Here are several practical methods for getting started:

1. Book Reviews: Getting your book reviewed on popular blogs is an effective way to get attention for your book from large centers of influence. Book Review blogs specifically offer a rich gathering of dedicated readers, hungry for the next book launch. Submitting your book to a review site is a great way to build momentum and get readers—and the search engines—to take notice.

2. Guest Blogger: Consider offering to submit a daily/weekly/monthly article to bloggers who are active in your niche. It is recommended that you keep an inventory of articles related to your book, in order to capitalize on this exposure.

There are massive numbers of blogs that accept review requests. Finding them can be a time-consuming process, so this is one task you may want to assign to a Virtual Assistant.

Whether you're flying solo or have an assistant, the process is the same. Start by researching relevant blogs to your topic. My method is to identify the top 100 bloggers within special interest groups. Once you have built your list, you will start contacting the administrators of the blog to inquire about Book Reviews or becoming a guest author on the blog.

One final note—you'll want to check the popularity of a blog by looking up the Alexa rank of the blog. The lower the ranking of the website, the more people are visiting that website (a low Alexa rank is a good thing).

In summary, to make the most of these methods, consider the following tips for content development.

- Create an inventory of articles that you can multi-purpose. Having an inventory of story ideas and topics can come in handy when you distribute your articles.

- Research high-traffic bloggers who relate to your topic. Ask them to become a guest author for you. Alternatively, you can arrange to become a guest on their blog.

- Use your articles as scripts in a podcast show. The most popular podcast length is about 15 to 30 minutes, and your text equates to about 10,000 words per hour.

- Many podcast shows are eager for guests. Research shows related to your topic and ask to be a guest on their show.

Where will your next book launch take you? With the potent combo of podcasting and blogs, you are well on your way to a successful book launch!

The Golden Egg: How to Work with a Public Relations Firm

The journey to a best-selling book often hinges on your skill working with a PR, or public relations firm. The author's path to fame and glory is strewn with brilliant ideas and wild goose chases. So many book promotion plans sound good on paper but turn out to be ineffectual.

There are authors who crack the code anew every day and wind up on the Best Seller list. So why not you? After all, every best-selling author has to start with a plan.

With this in mind, is it a good idea for an author to hire a PR firm to promote their published works? Like so many things, the answer isn't cut and dried. It all depends. While you nearly always get what you pay for, it's crucial to be clear about what exactly it is you're paying for when hiring an agency to promote your book.

The first thing to look at is your goal for promoting your book. Are you publishing your book so you can have the credibility of being a published author? If what you want is the respect of having this important credential, then releasing your book into the marketplace may well be enough. A few book release announcements on your blog and newsletter could give you some exposure. This means that with a "book release" instead of a "product launch," you can use your book as your calling card to get new speaking and consulting gigs.

But what if the credential of getting published is not enough? What about those ambitious authors who want their books to propel their brand to a nationwide audience?

Finding the right kind of help to tell your story to the media can make all the difference in the return on investment you get with your book release. This is the job of a book release PR firm.

Finding the Masses

Most authors invest months, even years of blood, sweat, toil and tears writing their manuscript. Ironically, many authors believe that if their book is good, it will sell itself. Have you looked at the volume of books on Amazon lately? Each year, there are hundreds of thousands of new books released... just in the non-fiction category! The idea that your book release is going to rise to the top of the sales charts based on the sheer brilliance contained within its pages is hopeful, at best.

A good book is certainly worth the effort of a good hearty launch. But how do you go about it? Using a skilled literary PR agency could be the answer to putting your message in front of your primary audience.

One of the biggest appeals of hiring a PR firm is the well-worn path they've trod to media outlets. A non-fiction author with the right platform is highly desirable in the eyes of talk show hosts, and a good PR firm knows just how to get their attention.

Popular topics like business, politics, finance, inspiration, health and relationships draw viewers and listeners to fresh ideas and the authors who write about them. If you've got a good story to tell, you could very well find yourself on TV or radio with the help of a solid PR firm.

Social media is also a key ingredient in your book publicity campaign. While it's up to you as an author to develop your following, a qualified PR firm can help you design an effective social media master plan. They can also direct you to other like-minded centers of influence in the social sphere. The degree of help with social media depends on the agency.

What Makes a Great Publishing PR Agency?

Whatever your level of experience—from first-time indie author to veteran bestseller—hiring a PR agency to market your book is probably a smart move. So, what do you look for? Here are the top 4 ingredients:

1. **Industry Specialization:** Often, a PR firm that has experience with media outlets which cover the topic of your book is the best place to start. A client of mine, Dr. Allan Colman, consults with marketing departments of law firms. He is working with a PR firm that is involved in the legal industry and has lists and current contacts with the influencers in this industry. Hence, the PR specialist knows about media outlets that an industry outsider would be hard-pressed to identify.

2. **Literary PR Agencies:** There are a variety of PR firms who work exclusively on book releases. This means that they are savvy to insider dynamics of working in the book trade. This can include managing things like:

   - Award Submissions: They keep a list of literary awards on-file and regularly submit manuscripts for consideration.

   - Trade Reviews: Book industry buyers read trade journals regularly. Reviews in the major literary trade journals have extraordinary weight on buying decisions from corporate buyers and library districts. Some of these respected journals include Publishers Weekly, Library Journal, and Kirkus.

   - Bookstore Tours: There is a list of highly respected bookstores nationwide, and some PR firms will maintain a list of people to contact for high-impact bookstore tours with large independent retailers including Powell's Books, Politics & Prose or Elliott Bay Bookstore.

- Speaking Tour: There are many speaking engagement opportunities which are available to authors, who are considered experts in their field.

3. **Dream Media Outlets**: Often successful authors will identify a list of dream media outlets where they want to expose their books. Provide this list to your PR firm and get their ideas on how to get featured in these publications.

4. **Weekly Reports to your Publisher**: Your publisher can work magic if you feed them real-time information about "PR wins." Feeding this information on a regular basis to their Sales and Marketing teams does wonders, as sales teams tend to talk-up books that are getting national media attention.

Take an unflinching look at the strength of your network of news outlets, blogs and book reviewers. The marketing support you get from your publishing agency will be greatly enhanced by the amount of time and attention you contribute to your success.

Be clear about the tasks you want to accomplish before hiring a PR firm. By getting clear about your goals and milestones before hiring an agency, you can be sure that the PR firm you hire will help you and your book reach the widest possible audience. Instead of a wild goose chase, you could end up with a basket of golden eggs!

6

Social Media & The Art
of Selling Books

LET'S face it: there are a boatload of creative promotional methods for driving book sales. Some methods are ingenious and highly effective. Others' methods... not so much.

The fact is there are many ways to spend your time to promote a book. If you're going to do social media, you need to be investing your time—not just spending it.

In book marketing circles, the pros in this business manage dozens of effective marketing tactics to support a book launch. Knowing that there are many different marketing options to choose from, the question then becomes this: which method offers the most bang for your buck? In other words, where can you get the highest return for the time or money you apply?

Without a doubt, one of the most obvious answers to this question is using social media to generate awareness and successfully promote your book. For many authors, marketing with social media is the new normal. In fact, it's so common that Presidential candidates relentlessly use social media networks for engaging their constituents. Often, their results are impressive when used in a manner that is consistent with the social network. For instance, what works on LinkedIn may not work on other social media networks.

When Social Media Works (and When It Doesn't)

Bottom line: social media is powerful. Social networks have allowed us to connect with friends and family around the world, discover innovative products, support cherished causes, and promote our ideas like never before. Whatever your fan base, you can get the word out about your most recent developments and reach a massive amount of people in seconds—if you use the right tactics.

Many pundits suggest using social media to promote books, but the rules keep changing in the industry. As the social media platforms focus more on profits, the opportunities to leverage these networks for low-cost exposure is shrinking. As the rules for posting content are changing rapidly, you just can't reach as many people as you used to.

For instance, some social media networks will not circulate your posts to all your fans unless you pay them to advertise your post. Some experts estimate that only 2% to 5% of your fans will see your posts. If you want to reach the rest, you will have to pay the social media company to advertise (or boost) the post to your fan base.

And what about the quality of that message? Whatever you post needs to be a) in-line with your message; b) an enhancement to your reputation; or c) unique enough to inspire sharing. Anything less could be detrimental to your personal brand.

For example, if your book is about wildlife photography, you could turn off your fan base when your dinner companion posts a photo of the wild elk special you are trying in Park City at Robert Redford's wild game restaurant. Think before you post, and make it count. You won't get a second chance if you screw it up.

What is Your Time Worth?

If you are already in motion using social media and love it, then leveraging social media is a great tool to promote your book. Go for it, and use the medium to showcase your writing, post images, and share video. You have every reason to take advantage of this ubiquitous tool.

However, the reality is that social media can be pretty time-consuming. Making the most of social media marketing means being consistent with your scheduling and your topics. If you're posting comments, images and videos at off-peak hours for your fan base, you're singing in the wind. Use one of the many apps available to analyze your fan base and see when your friends and followers are online. Post your most valuable pieces during those times.

Likewise, look at the best use of your time as an author working towards building a platform for your book release. If you're committed to accessing your platform with social media, consider hiring an assistant or social media manager to help you stay in stride.

Video is hugely effective, so don't ignore this opportunity. Video posts get phenomenal circulation, and they are rapidly taking over social media sites such as Facebook. It goes without saying that YouTube is the monster in the room here, with billions of hours of new video posted each month. The funnier your video, the better the circulation you can expect.

In the end, all that counts is that you push your message to your public by whatever means you have at your disposal. There are countless authors who have written successful book launches without a social media presence. They confide in me that they read articles telling them they must use social media to promote their books. However, they were able to use other methods to promote their work successfully.

Is this true? Will your writing career tank if you don't feed the social media monster at breakfast, lunch, and dinner? Is the only path to success to climb on the bandwagon and do what everyone else is doing?

Absolutely not! There are so many ways to invest your time and promote your book. Social media is just one of the many marketing tactics to support a book launch. Though all promotional activities require either time or money to implement, you have to choose what fits your book the best. As an author, you can let your creativity guide you to your best marketing options.

However, one truism holds fast: unless you get the word out, no one will know what gems of knowledge your book holds. Start beating your own drum today, and reap the rewards tomorrow.

Social Media, Book Promotion and the Sweet Smell of Success

Ah, the sweet smell of success: your book is finally a household name, the topic of conversation in coffee houses and the subject of toasts in fine dining establishments. Just yesterday, you turned down a media interview due to your busy schedule. Tomorrow you're off to Barbados for a quick dip in the salty surf, then a date with a rum-laced umbrella drink under a palm tree. Lucky you!

Or was it luck? Maybe it was all that time you put in on social media, carefully cultivating relationships with your fans and followers. You lost track of how many late nights you spent loading up your Buffer account, cheese popcorn crumbs littering the front of your PJ's like dandruff.

"Oh, if they could see me now," you mutter, catching a sideways glimpse in the mirror. Whatever happened to that polished look you cultivated so carefully for your book jacket? Gone is the mohair suit and carefully waxed hairstyle. "Uff, it's a good thing I'm not on my webcam..." you say under your breath.

But in reality, checking in with your fans doesn't have to mean looking polished all the time. Unlike days gone by, you don't necessarily have to show your face to sell a lot of books.

The thing about promoting yourself (and your book) on social media is that you can literally do the work anywhere you choose to be. The magic combination of a solid manuscript, the right book cover and a good social media promotion campaign can put your readership over the top. It just takes a little planning and a couple of good tools; then you're off to the races! Or the sands of the Caribbean. Whatever.

Social media sites are the most efficient and cost-effective way to get your message in front of potentially millions of people. Google's $1.6 billion purchase of YouTube and Facebook's multi-billion dollar IPO shouted a wake-up call to anyone who'd been hitting that marketing snooze button. There's good reason for these high price tags; social networks offer a pool teaming with commercial opportunity for major players and individuals alike. As a published author, this opportunity now includes you. The playing field is about as level as it gets.

As an author, you can leverage the ready-made audiences on social media. This means you can get involved with groups that either are tailored to your audience or dovetail nicely with your topic. Take a look at how big publishing companies are using social media to promote their top authors, then borrow a page from their playbook.

Using Social Media to Generate Social Proof

Social media helps you generate what marketers call "social proof."

Publishing your carefully cultivated testimonials from your readers can build the bond of trust for your would-be fans and their immediate social circles. The psychology of word-of-mouth testimonials is a powerful ally for authors who don't yet have huge brand awareness. According to a survey by eMarketer, an overwhelming 99% of people surveyed believe that testimonials are credible and influence their buying decisions.

To leverage social proof online, follow these 3 steps:

1. **Clearly understand your target audience**—both their demographics and psychographics. Who are they? Get clear about their age, income, location, family life, interests and peeves. Find out what makes them hurt and what gives them pleasure.

2. **Create messaging and imagery** that is consistent with your target audience. For instance, if you are targeting empty nesters who are between 50 and 63 years old, you would use inspirational messages and images consistent with their outlook. In this case, you might use imagery of happy grandchildren, RV travel to national parks, beach vacations, spas or wine tasting.

3. **Pick your "call to action" campaign strategies** from options that are consistent with your target audience's lifestyle. Then consider which techniques will influence their buying behavior. Do you want them to take a

survey? Tell their friends? Watch a video and comment on it? Get creative, and keep your audience involved.

Keep Your Message in Front of Your Fans with a Book Marketing Timeline

You can increase your sales and your free time by creating a social media campaign timeline. Timelines are essential, and all successful authors use them to organize social media campaigns. Some authors even use their timelines to set and track their campaign goals.

Come up with your present and future goals, along with action plans for today, tomorrow and next month. Have a method for tracking sales so you can see what's working for you. Pick a few social media networks to focus your activity, and post to them 2 to 3 times a day. Increase this frequency for the 3 weeks on either side of your book launch, and stay interested in how people are responding to you and your message.

It may seem like a bit of work to pack in, but there are plenty of automation tools such as Buffer.com or HootSuite that can help you manage the workload. You can pre-write an inventory of Facebook posts or Twitter tweets in advance and load-up your free Buffer account to stimulate engagement with your readers.

That means you can be active on social media even when you're sipping an umbrella drink on the beach on a remote tropical island. Just don't eat popcorn while you're there on the sand, lying in the sun… the crumbs can make for a spotty tan. Cheers!

Book Marketing with Facebook Ads – Who Says You Can't Buy Happiness?

The tale is almost as ancient as writing itself. Picture the author in an ancient Italian city, scribbling away into the night by the dim amber light of a candle. He peeks out his window in a garret above the crowded street below—one teeming with readers he hopes to entertain, influence, convince or transform.

His livelihood depends on it. Somehow he must overcome obscurity and get his book into the hands of as many readers as possible. As an author, he must reach them to survive.

Fast forward to the 21st century, and—BLAM!—a burst of light explodes onto the scene in the form of technology. It spreads like wildfire to the far corners of the world in the span of a decade.

The garret is now a home office in outer suburbia, and the crowded street is replaced with a finely edged lawn. Ink spilled from a quill becomes the glow from a tablet, spread at the touch of a button to a prospective audience of billions through Audible and Kindle. Friends and followers who were once as far away as the moon are now brought near through social networks, online video and video conferencing.

In the history of the world, authors have never had it so good. Yet with so much opportunity available to everyone, the ancient question remains unchanged: how do you stand out?

As an author, how do you keep your family (and your banker) happy, and reach those teeming masses of readers? The answer may surprise you and is not a closely held "secret" as some would have you to believe.

Reaching a Massive Audience

Twenty years ago, social networks had more than their fair share of social misfits. As AOL was supplanted by MySpace, the color and candor of the scene started to change. It became mainstream. In the era of Facebook, Twitter and YouTube, social media has gradually become reason enough for late adopters to join the world online.

Social media networks keep your message in front of the consumer. But how do you do this if you don't have an established list of followers? Reaching out to like-minded people one-by-one on social networks isn't the way to reach large numbers of people. If you join a Facebook group and post something that says, "Buy now and save!" you'll get no response—and may even get banned from the group.

Paid advertising on these networks is an efficient way to reach the people who want and need your book. It puts the power into the hands of the author. This spells opportunity to connect with far more than your immediate social circles as well, and that makes everyone happy: your friends, your family, your banker—and especially you, the author!

Over the years, marketing tools come and go. Smartphones and social media have changed the landscape of marketing in ways no one could have predicted. The next disruption is right around the corner. Regardless of the latest marketing technologies, there are three principles that have held true for decades.

1. **Audience Targeting:** Segment your audiences, and cater your efforts just to the buyers. Clearly identify what makes them tick (emotionally).

   Consider going beyond old-fashioned demographic segmentation and look for patterns in personality types. Take, for example, two 45-year-old women that live in the same city—one is a successful real estate professional, and one is the CEO of a software company. Would the same advertising appeal to one woman who is motivated by building a massive network versus another woman who is focused on leading software development?

   Paid social media advertising offers some of the best audience targeting opportunities ever afforded by the marketing community. No longer do we target large blocks of unsegmented people via network television buys. Now, authors can easily target readers based on where they live, age, gender, books they have read and movies they watch.

2. **Multiple Campaigns:** If you're launching one marketing campaign at a time, you won't get very far. In today's climate, your offer will need to cater to multiple audiences simultaneously. This may require launching multiple marketing campaigns with highly specific targeting. Taking the example of targeting the two women, perhaps one campaign targeting the real estate professional is themed around entertaining

while another campaign is geared towards leadership education.

3. **Specialized Messaging:** Your promotional messaging can't be a catch-all for multiple audiences. Using a catch-all philosophy only "catches" a few. Profile your target audiences to increase conversion rates from your offers.

Take a look at your ideal audience and identify their greatest pain and their biggest pleasure. Then apply these pressure points when designing your social media campaigns for higher conversions.

You may think that paying for advertising isn't necessary for your business, but in the final analysis, when do you want to succeed—now, or someday? Are you enjoying the warm amber glow of that dim candle, or would you like to explode your book awareness from the comfort of your suburban office?

Opportunity doesn't wait. With sound advertising practices, you can apply leverage to your book marketing campaigns and invest your time wisely somewhere else—say, edging that finely manicured lawn.

7

How to Profit from Bookstore Signings

A tried and true method of selling books is to schedule a series of bookstore signings. One successful author wrote a book on her experience in Girl Scouts called *Under Their Wings*, then scheduled bookstore signings across the nation. Local chapters of Girl Scouts engaged with the author to fill the room, and the author proceeded to sell thousands of books in mega-bookstore chains.

Doing bookstore appearances correctly is an art form and can be perfected with the process outlined in this chapter. When you show up professionally, you can expect amazing results in raising awareness for your book in a venue that matters most—in bookstores.

Some experts question the value of doing bookstore signings. For some, they can be a zero-sum game. However, if you study the techniques and steps in this chapter, you'll be spending your time in a profitable manner. This method has proven to be an effective method for first-time authors in selling over 10,000 books at retail. Now it's your turn!

Bookstore Signings: Are They Profitable or Like Chasing a Unicorn?

Is it worth it for an author to do a book signing tour? As a publisher, this question is often raised. Authors want to know if they should invest the time and effort in a meet-and-greet with their readers, and what exactly the payoff is. With so many options for promotion—from social media to social climbing—narrowing the field of marketing activities to promote a book only makes sense.

It's a great question, and the answer is usually a resounding yes. However, it all depends on what you want to get out of a book signing. Not all authors see the value in it, and with good reason. It takes a bit of imagination and a view of the big picture to understand where benefits are from a bookstore signing event. A single event won't reveal the big picture.

I recall having a good-natured debate about this topic with an author the other day over coffee. This author has published more than a hundred titles. Like many authors, she believes that the amount of work involved in putting on a great event just doesn't pay off. She says the effort could be better spent on online promotion; one of her specialties. Staring into her latte, she told me, "A great book signing is like a unicorn—it's tough to find, and even harder to bring home."

This sounds poetic, but the idea itself is a myth. Book signings do work. This author's experience with individual bookstore signings events has been at par, closing 10% of the room. But, it barely pays for a nice lunch at a place where they set the table with fine crystal and linen. However, it's the intangibles of the book signings that put the author's career in motion and move books by the carton. Let's explore this a little further.

When Do You Want to Score – Now or Never?

In reality, the success of your publicity as an author depends most of all on consistency. It's like a well-played game of baseball. If you hit a home run once in a while, you may win occasionally. But you're more likely to win consistently with a series of solid base hits. I parried this back to an author who specializes in online marketing, and she yawned. "Give me a handful of golden keywords," she said, "and I'll show you some base hits." It's hard to argue with the amount of passive income she's generated from online promotions. One of her programs was a best-seller one summer—five years after it was launched.

Whether or not the path to success is paved with the sublime or the mundane, success is success. Many major keynote speakers I represent have consistently done book signing events in bookstores. I'll give you a case in point and the reason to do local appearances.

Another author, Bill Chandler, uses book signings to great effect. In fact, he used local events to sell over 10,000 copies of his book, "The Ultimate Inventors Handbook." Bill is not a boring guy, and neither is he bored by book signings.

Bill's background as a marketing professor helps because he understands the psychological dynamics of mass-market buying behavior. "Works like a charm," he told me over a steak salad, dabbing the corners of his mouth with a unicorn-white cloth napkin. Moreover, Bill's experience gives us every reason to talk about book signings as a worthy tool for promotion.

Tracking the Success of Your Book Signings

Organizing a tour of bookstores is time-consuming. When you look at the hard cost of trading your time for book sales, a book signing can mean a high cost per lead—especially if your event is under-attended. Nobody wants to be "that author" sitting behind a table in a bookstore with no line, no fans and not a single book sold.

Yet it happens more often than you might think. So where's the payoff? What's the point in expending all that energy just to sell five books? What if the only attendees who are buying include your mom, your best friends and a few neighbors?

Ah, but not so fast. There is magic in book signings, and they can turn a dull career into a sparkling magical beast. What many authors don't realize is that 82% of books are purchased through word of mouth. When a trusted friend reads a book, they tell others. This is one dynamic that makes book signings a very smart move for authors.

Book signings pay off in the following ways:

1. **Drumming up book sales**: Use book signings to increase your in-store book sales. Besides rubbing elbows with your community, you will also encourage readers to talk it up with their friends.

2. **Book buyer relationships**: Bookstore buyers are people too, and they want to put a face to the names on the spines they buy. If you can deliver buzz to their store, they are much more likely to stock their shelves consistently with your books. If you know what you are doing, bookstores may request unsold inventory to be signed by the author, which is merchandised on a special table in bookstores. This will bring in sales long after the day of the event and give you premium shelf space in the bookstore.

3. **Creating media momentum**: This is the single greatest benefit of book signings. Local media interviews and other publicity around your event can generate significant momentum for your book sales. Even though you may only sell a handful of books on the day of the event, the media publicity you generate will bolster your reputation and your book sales. My friend Bill likes to focus energies on one major city at a time until he has accomplished exposure in three key cities across three states. This can be enough to get the ball of momentum rolling fast enough to sell 10,000 books.

Book signings can be an incredible tool for boosting your book sales and your career as an author. Authors who commit the effort must also be gifted with imagination, but the payoff is as fine and rarefied as a unicorn.

10 Step Roadmap to Successful Bookstore Signings

Organizing a tour of bookstores is time-consuming, so this question comes up often with authors. The last thing we want is you sitting in front of an empty table. Yet it happens more often than you think.

So what can you do to make a book signing rock?

The formula I'm about to share was created by the aforementioned author Bill Chandler, which he used to sell over 10,000 copies of his book "*The Ultimate Inventors Handbook.*" This was not a vampire novel, nor a romance novel. This is a formula used successfully for a book targeting inventors.

Bill's background as a Marketing Professor helps, as he understands the psychological dynamics of buying behavior. But one day, Bill was "that author"... Bill was sitting behind his book table in the middle of a busy mall for one hour, without a single person talking to him. How embarrassing! Not to mention an incredible waste of time.

So, to save you from this situation, here is a 10-step formula for doing book signings. Remember, however, that you MUST complete all 10 steps to make this formula work for your book signings. There are no shortcuts to success in this endeavor.

1. Call a local bookstore and schedule your signing 3 months in advance. Be prepared to talk up your book. It is possible to book a signing with a 5-day lead-time, but this is not ideal.

2. Barnes & Noble stores have a designated "CRM" in each store who organizes author signing events. Ask for the CRM at the front desk or by phone when setting up your event.

3. After scheduling your date, send your contact your author bio, photo, cover artwork, ISBN and a description of your book. The book industry has a standard template for this information called a Tip Sheet. Contact your publisher to request the Tip Sheet for your book.

4. Contact local radio stations and newspapers in the area of the bookstore and send them a Press Release with the details of your book signings. Be persistent!

5. Create a list of questions for media interviewers (radio and TV), along with a topic of interest to talk about. The more current or controversial is always a good bet with the media.

6. Check in with the bookstore to ensure they have produced flyers promoting your signing.

7. Message your friends, clients and contacts about your event. Call, email and make social media posts to spread the word. Ensure at least 10-20 friends/family/co-workers/fans/clients show up. There is power in a crowd, and a crowd draws a crowd! When you bring a crowd, the bookstore will love you.

8. Get to the store one hour before your signing, and personally hand out postcards talking about your book. Invite shoppers to join you at your signing time and tell them where to go. It is recommended to bring

an assistant who can also hand out cards, right before you share your talk outlined in #10.

9. Personally get on the In-Store Announcement system to call people to your table.

10. Deliver your well-rehearsed 20-minute speech about your book, tell some stories and do a reading from your book. Make your book visible to the crowd while you speak. Some authors insist on holding a copy of their book while they speak.

    Give people the opportunity to take home a signed copy of your book at the end of your speech. Taking home a signed book is highly valuable to the general public. Remember this, as this is the most important part of this formula: ask for the order and don't be shy.

But wait, you're not done yet! The key to this formula is to schedule multiple store signings within a 2 to 3-week period, with the emphasis on Steps #3 & #4 above. The repetition of your message is the magic, and you'll find that the 2nd or 3rd time people hear about you and your book, they get more responsive and more willing to buy.

Branding Axiom: 7 brand impressions lead to trust. Trust leads to purchase behavior.

Once you have saturated the bookstores in one market, then move to the next market (such as a neighboring city).

As 82% of books are purchased via Word of Mouth, you can get the momentum rolling when one person reads a book; then they tell others. This is how books become Best Sellers. Plain and simple.

By performing these 10 steps in several markets, you can cross the Critical Marketing Threshold and will get a snowball of momentum started with your work across the country.

Bookstore Signing Checklist

1. **What to wear:**

   Business casual dress, and/or whatever is appropriate for the genre of your book. For example: cute red dress for romance writer, suit and tie for CEO, t-shirt for a young technology expert, cowboy hat and jeans for the western novelist.

2. **When to arrive:**

   Arrive 60 minutes prior to your scheduled book talk and stay 30 minutes after.

3. **What to bring:**

   - Three (3) black permanent marker pens (Sharpies)
   - Work with the store on a pre-order of books or bring consignment inventory
   - Bookmarks, postcards or other marketing collateral
   - List of Reader's Reviews

- Speaker One Sheet

- Laptop or Tablet to display book or speaker website

- Extension cord and power strip

- Pop-up banner

- Author Introduction – a short 25-word introduction that the bookstore manager can read to introduce you to the crowd

4. **Prepare your "book talk":**

    a. Deliver a well-rehearsed 15 to 30-minute presentation about your book. Tell some stories and do a reading from your book. Make your book visible to the crowd while you speak. This is your chance to convince the crowds why they cannot possibly survive without owning your book and buying another as a gift.

    b. Allow time at the end of your event for crowd interaction and questions.

5. **Interact:**

    a. Don't just sit at the table. Don't wait for them to come to you. Be the store's official greeter while you are there. Walk around the store with several copies of your book and introduce yourself to everyone. I know that this is not easy for everyone, so consider bringing an extroverted friend to help out. Oftentimes, one of the store employees can help with this task if you ask them nicely.

    b. When people stop by the table, one trick that author Scott Hogle (a sales professional) shared is that he will hand them a copy of his book as he is introducing himself. Scott reports that people will almost always take to book with them. Tell them to look at it and bring it back to the table when they are finished. If they begin to read it, that's your cue to keep quiet. On average, books sales have been tripled at signings by implementing this tip as once people have a product in their hand, they are likely to purchase it!

c. As an author, you should *always* sign your books. Some people are too shy to ask for your autograph. Sign it anyway! Simply ask, "Here, let me sign that for you. Whose name would you like in it?" Always ask.

6. **Other Tips:**

a. **Bring a speaker one-sheet.** Be sure the information lists all published titles, where your books can be purchased and a website where readers may go to for more information or to purchase your books. Include that you are available for public appearances and speaking engagements and list your appropriate contact information.

b. **Have copies of reader's reviews available at your table.** Hand them to anyone who shows the least bit of interest in your book and say, "Here's what other people who have read my books have to say." Make extra copies for giveaways. When someone begins to read the reviews, remain quiet. Amazon. com can be a good source where people post impartial reviews of your book.

c. **Have an attractive two-color or four-color bookmark** designed by a graphic artist and print a thousand of them. You can give one to everyone who comes in the store. List a few endorsements on it as well as a brief paragraph of what the book is about. Include the URL of your author website. Perhaps include an Endorsement or two on the bookmark. Put the price and the ISBN on your bookmark.

d. **Give something away** (anything, except your book—don't give the book away, you want them to buy a copy). Have visitors sign a "guestbook" or "free drawing" card with their name, e-mail address and phone number to qualify. Announce the winner at the end of your book signing. People love the idea of a chance to win something free, and it often causes them to linger in the store longer. Think about creating a mug with your cover artwork for giveaways.

With this formula for bookstore signings, every event you do will be a success. The event will feel natural and you don't have to be "salesy" to have a great series of bookstore signing events.

8

How to Promote a Book on Goodreads

IF promoting your book online from the comfort of your home office sounds appealing, then having a Goodreads strategy is just the ticket for you. In this chapter, we will explore the largest social media network dedicated to readers, Goodreads.com. By understanding what it is, coupled with strategies for becoming a credible voice in this network of readers, you can capitalize on this opportunity to promote your book on your own terms.

In this chapter, we will explore the fundamentals of Goodreads, how to promote effectively, and a step-by-step approach to organizing your time.

Goodreads for Authors: Reflections on Fundamentals

"Gentlemen, this is a football." Vince Lombardi famously spoke these words to his team when he took over as head coach of the Green Bay Packers in 1959. While it's probably true that the players he was speaking to were well aware of the ball's name, reinforcing the fundamentals never hurt anybody.

In fact, the Packers went on to unprecedented victory under Lombardi's leadership because of his relentless drills on the fundamentals. The Packers became champions many times over, helping football to become the national mania it is today. The Super Bowl trophy is known as the Vince Lombardi cup, and winning it is a testament to the team's ability to master the basics.

So what does this have to do with you as an author and the success of your book marketing? It's simple: if you want to succeed, you must never stop reviewing the fundamentals. Return to bedrock as often as you can. Honing your book marketing skills in just a few basic areas can launch your career and keep it aloft for a long time to come.

As an author, one of the most basic steps you can take to promote your book is to be present places where the readers show up. This means a portion of your promotional time needs to be focused on Goodreads.com. Not only is this good for you, but it's good for the millions of Goodreads members who are wondering what to read next. Unlike some social media sites, this is one place where your book promotions are not only okay; people are hungry for them.

Simple Does Not Mean Stupid

Goodreads has a simple premise: it's a free membership site devoted to books and book lovers. It was started back in 2007 with the intent of allowing readers to make book recommendations. Since then, the site has grown to over 41 million members with nearly 300 million page views per month. That's a whole lot of eyeballs.

This makes Goodreads the biggest book club on the planet, and getting involved in it is a smart move for you as an author. The average members are well-off, educated professionals— mostly women—with a deep-seated passion for the written word. They work in fields like Education, Law and Market Research, which means they're pretty sharp cookies. You don't have to worry about talking over their heads.

Still, just because this is the average reader profile, that doesn't mean you can't find other bookish types on the site— men, women, young, old, rich, poor, conservative or woo-woo. The sheer number of members means you can find just about any kind of group you'd like to reach, with tastes that range from Horror to Humor and from Self Help to Sci-Fi. Whatever you've written, Goodreaders are likely to give your material a fair assessment.

Once you're a member of Goodreads, you can engage in their Author Program. This status is free, and it allows you to take advantage of the rich pool of avid readers and hungry buyers to promote your magnum opus. Upgrading your status from a standard member to an Author means submitting an application to Goodreads' staff for review. You should hear back from them in a couple of days, so sit tight. It will definitely be worth the wait.

Here are 10 fundamentals to have ready when you set up your Goodreads account:

1. Book Title
2. Subtitle
3. Description
4. ISBN
5. Cover artwork
6. Author photo
7. Author bio
8. Links to other social media accounts
9. Link to your website
10. Link to your blog (an RSS feed is preferred to automatically keep your blog posts current on Goodreads)

Whether you want to participate in group discussions, create a Book Giveaway, or advertise on the site, the sheer numbers of this social media giant make it fundamental to your book promotion campaign.

Goodreads Advertising: How it Works

When it comes to talking about the fundamentals of book promotion, using Goodreads is about as fundamental as you can get. Can 41 million readers be wrong? Probably not. With that in mind, here are steps you can take to maximize the return on your investment of time and attention to your book marketing campaigns.

The Goodreads Trifecta of Promotion

1. **Community & Good Citizenship:** Get involved in the Goodreads community, and when your book is released, ask people to review it on the site. As a member of the Goodreads community, you'll want to observe decorum. Use the same common courtesies you would in any other online social setting. Take a week or so to observe the tone and the content of threads within the groups. When you feel confident that you've got the knack, start participating by leaving considered comments. Once you become a bit more known, you can create threads of your own. After you've become a trusted member of the community, you can add your book title or have someone add it for you. This gradual approach means you are less likely to look like an amateur and more likely to be considered a respected voice in the community.

2. **Book Giveaways:** Once you're established on Goodreads.com, you can create buzz and get reviews by giving away free copies of your book. To do this, click the Goodreads link to "Create A Giveaway." These are physical books you're giving away, so you'll need to have copies of your book on hand to send to reviewers who request it. Be sure you conduct only

one giveaway at a time, or this can get expensive and confusing. Some experts suggest allocating 25 books to Goodreads Giveaways, and running multiple giveaway campaigns over a period of time. With that said, this is an excellent way to generate the best kind of publicity for your book—word of mouth.

3. **Paid Advertising:** Goodreads advertising means you can reach an ultra-targeted market for an incredibly low investment. Here is real data from an ad run on Goodreads. The budget was $49, but in actuality we only spent $1 on the total campaign in 30 days. This cost may seem like it's too low to be effective, but the ad for the book generated 13,300 impressions. Because there were only two click-throughs, there was virtually no cost to the author for this phenomenal exposure. Where I come from in the world of book marketing, this is an astonishing amount of reach for very little expense.

Following are the stats for the ad, promoting the book "Gotcha" by Dr. Sally Earnst.

- **Daily Views**: 181

- **Daily Clicks**: 0

- **Daily Cost**: $0.00

- **Total Views**: 13,300

- **Total Clicks**: 2

- **Total Cost**: $1.00

Where else can you produce 31,000 book exposures for a buck? Promoting your book is fundamental to your success as an author, and leveraging the power of Goodreads makes it an easy call.

Goodreads Giveaways:
Step by Step Instructions

Have you ever had one of those moments when you just felt "on it"? On top of the world? In the zone? You know what I mean… it's that feeling you get watching Bruno Mars singing those lyrics during Super Bowl 50: "Too hot. Hot damn!" Maybe it was one of those good hair days. You were wearing your favorite "go to" shirt and a new pair of Italian loafers. You had an answer for everything—people just wanted to hang around you.

Or maybe you've had that experience where you went to an event and clicked so thoroughly with the folks around you, it turned out you were the most popular person in the room. Your best joke had a cadre of eager listeners in a tight shoulder-to-shoulder semi-circle, edged forward and waiting for you to deliver the punchline like a swift uppercut.

By the end of the evening, you'd clinched a new deal, had four new phone numbers and a box seat for next weekend's big game. At the midnight hour, just before you went home, all of you toasted to good health. A glow seemed to follow you out the door, settling like a mist under the chassis of your car as you drove away while humming "Happy" by Pharrell Williams.

Whether this is a page from your everyday life or it's something you've never even thought of going after, this kind of experience is available to you as an author when you find your groove. It's the kind of thing that could happen to you when you put your book in front of a thirsty crowd of readers on Goodreads.

Get Your Groove On

Goodreads is a social network started by readers and dedicated to the proposition that the best books are the ones your friends recommend. In short, if you're an author, it's the best place in the world for you to be.

When you show up on Goodreads and give away autographed copies of your book, you're sure to be in your groove. Here's a step-by-step guide to using Goodreads giveaways to promote your book.

Let's Take It Step-by-Step

Building excitement and anticipation for your book release is a job of every author on the planet. Using sweepstakes and giveaways on Goodreads is a great method to build anticipation and generate positive Reviews on Amazon and Goodreads.

You must recognize that there is a cost associated with putting your book in front of potential devoted fans. However, this type of promotion is much more effective and economical than paying for advertising. It also puts you in that rare category of "life of the party." Here is a 7-step recipe for running a Goodreads giveaway:

1. **First, create an account on Goodreads.com.** Get familiar with the site, and start making comments in relevant groups when you feel comfortable with the venue. Make sure you adhere to common guidelines of forum etiquette.

2. **Sign up to be recognized as an author** by the Goodreads team. This requires approval, which can take a couple of days, but hang in there. It's worth it.

3. **Host a giveaway** on Goodreads to put your book in the hands of thirsty readers. These are physical copies of your book, and they are always autographed. When people ask for them, respond quickly, courteously and thoroughly.

4. **Write a description** for your giveaway that sounds juicy and makes people want to get their hands on your rare fare. Use excerpts from reviews to lure people in, and avoid using a book synopsis of a blurb from your back cover.

5. **Get the schedule right.** Like they say, what's the secret of comedy...? Timing! And just as skill with a well-timed joke can make you the toast of the town, a well-timed Goodreads giveaway can boost your publishing success. Schedule your giveaway for a future date, and build excitement for the event. Don't just release it; launch it.

6. **Keep your giveaway open** for just a couple days. This means your giveaway will be listed on the New

Giveaways and the Ending Giveaways at the same time—double exposure for a picture-perfect finish. Regardless of length, end your giveaway on a date that doesn't have a lot of other giveaways ending. Everyone else likes to end their promotions at the end of the month or national holidays like Thanksgiving or the Fourth of July. If you extend yours beyond these dates, your giveaway will rise to the top of the Ending Giveaways list and give you greater exposure.

7. **Keep it pretty.** Make sure your book cover is solid, and your synopsis is excellent. More than any other features of your book, these two things will close the deal for you. Also, the more reviews you have, the more book sales you will make. If your book giveaway looks lonely, it is sure to stay that way. Keep it attractive, and you are sure to be the life of the virtual party.

There you have it—the key to good times on Goodreads. Now you can take these steps, apply them, and be sure your book giveaway is a winner. If you're like many successful authors, once you get into motion promoting your book, then opportunities start to fall into place organically.

9

How to Build
an Author Website

AN author or speaker website can be an important tool in communicating your brand and your message. Knowing the essential elements of an author/speaker website will get you started on a path to spread your message without even leaving your home office.

However, if you've never built a website before, authors often ask "Where do I start?" This chapter is informed through building several hundred websites for authors, speakers and mega-companies. The process can be a little technical, so where I start is writing a Design Brief for a website, which then gets handed off to a web developer to implement. By working with a pro, you can spend your time more efficiently than learning how to code in HTML or website hosting logistics.

To find an experienced web developer, start by visiting freelancer websites like UpWork.com to search for qualified freelancers.

How to Make Your Author Website the "In" Place to Be

Once upon a time, when books were only printed on the static page, the conversation was more like a monologue. This meant the author's career was a bit like a college lecture on, say, frog dissection. It was a lonely, dusty, echoey place to be. I mean, who wants to wake up and smell the formaldehyde? Not fun. Not fun at all.

Even as recently as a decade ago, there was little chance for a reader to get involved in an author's work except by writing to the author, or maybe showing up at a lecture or book signing. Thankfully, all that has changed.

In the age of digits and downloads, the author's website is, well... electric, and even electrifying. Now it's more like a hip coffeehouse, or a dinner of nouvelle cuisine at 10:00 pm. It's become a busy hub for a wide array of content and media—interactive and highly actionable.

This shift in dynamic may seem obvious, but it's overlooked more often than it should be—much to the detriment of the author. If you're not sure where your own author website falls on the scale between humdrum and howling—between frog dissection and sautéed frogs' legs—these tips may lend you just the clue you're looking for.

Whisper—You Don't Have to Shout

Does your website shout at readers with a dozen or more calls to action? You want to involve them, not confuse them. The adage from the advertising world is to direct a Visitor's attention to just one thing, with one "Call to Action" message. Make sure your website is easy to use, with just the right balance between form and function.

Focus on content over design. You want a crisp, clean look with one clear call to action. Still, the substance of your message is more important than the look and feel, so keep the bells and whistles to a minimum. Don't use Flash if you can help it (due to mobile phone limitations), and trim your images to a manageable size before adding them to your posts. Let the site load time be fast and light.

The intent of your website should focus on the reader, not on you. Yes, this is your website, but you're not the one using it. It's all about your readers and what you can do for them.

Use your About page for boasts, toasts, testimonials and kudos. Keep the rest of the site focused on your reader. Have a tab for book news and reviews, offer a newsletter, and make sure you're easy to contact—things that show you're not only aware of their presence, but you're glad they came.

Think of your role as something like being the gracious host of a great party. If you just talk about yourself, you'll only inspire a lot of yawns, and folks may decide to turn in early or head to the shindig down the block. Instead, present your guests with a scintillating array of topics to nibble on. Also, introduce them to other personalities they may enjoy, and get the conversation going.

When someone shows up at your site, offer them exclusive unpublished content that they can't get anywhere else. Give them juicy morsels they would gladly pay for, like a short video, podcast episodes, short fiction, white papers, explainers and sample chapters.

Create content worth sharing; something your readers will discuss over coffee or happy hour with their incredibly interesting friends.

How to Keep Readers Coming Back for More

Be generous. Whose work do you read or recommend? Why is it worth anyone's precious free time? Support your peers and your fans at the same time. Shine a spotlight on people and topics that might not otherwise cross your reader's path.

Be human. Talk about your works in progress, and share the biggest triumphs and trials you have in the writing process. Are you stuck on one idea? Did you just shift the gender of your lead character and now you have to rewrite half your book? Did you suddenly realize that your magnum opus on finding happiness is really more about finding faith? Are you simply bored with the sound of your own voice and can't wait to finish your manuscript? Let your readers peek behind the curtain.

Be social. Encourage your readers to promote your fresh content on social media, and make it easy to do. For example, you can use the free service at

ClickToTweet.com to socialize your blog content. Summarize the topic of your blog post into about 100 characters, and include your ClickToTweet link. This will automatically post your headline, witty comment or quip to Twitter. For added link juice, use a hashtag.

Encourage comments on your blog and get involved with the conversation. In fact, why not encourage comments on the comments to build a real sense of community?

With a slight shift in focus, you can transform your author website from a dusty lecture hall into a roaring success.

The Top 4 Components of a Successful Author Website

Knowing where to start with the components of your author website makes the task of building your website a snap. Use this checklist as a starting point in the layout of your website.

1. **Home Page**: This is where you promote your Brand and the ideals that you represent.

2. **Book**: Create a dedicated page for your book with all the pertinent information about your book, which includes:

   a. Front Cover

   b. Description

    c. The price of the book, or the MSRP (Manufacturers Suggested Retail Price)

    d. ISBN

    e. Links to stores where people can purchase the book

    f. Short author biography

    g. Include an excerpt from the book, or a key quote or two

    h. List a few of your most high-impact endorsements

3. **About**: Include your bio, background and credentials. Don't overlook this page, as it is often the #1 link people click when they visit a new website.

4. **Contact Page**: Make yourself accessible to your readers. It is recommended to have a Contact form where people can submit requests that are emailed to you. If you are active on social media, include links to the social media pages where you are active.

10

Book Awards and Professional Reviews

ONE of the most powerful sources of exposure an author can achieve is winning writing awards and professional reviews. Why is this? The credential of a respected third party carries tremendous weight in the minds of readers as they contemplate which book to invest in reading for the next few weeks.

A book award can be in the format of a writing competition, where a panel of judges reviews books that are submitted. Winning an award has many benefits and can often be just the thing a book needs to get a second look by the book industry gatekeepers (book buyers, merchandisers, etc.).

But what is the difference between a book award and a professional review? A professional review is often written by a respected source which is read widely by book industry insiders to get an executive summary of your book's merits.

Let's explore the mechanics of these buzzworthy book marketing tactics!

Book Awards – Resting on Your Laurels and Other Thoughts on Winning Book Writing Competitions

Competing for a writing award is an often-overlooked tactic in the book marketing list of "To-Dos." But is it worth it? Let's take a look.

Back in the day—I mean way back—citizens of the Greek Empire knew they had made it big when they were crowned with a wreath made from bay laurel leaves. You know the kind: the pungent herb you use to season your holiday bird.

The ancient Greeks used laurel wreaths as awards for accomplishments in sports as well as poetry. Later on, the Romans copied the Greek custom and awarded laurels to victorious conquering generals. Judging from the size of the Roman Empire, they must have gone through a lot of leaves. Eventually, the generals got lazy, a lot of internal squabbling happened, and the empire declined. So too did the custom of awarding laurels.

Laurel wreaths are still used today as the symbol of academic success, and they're sometimes used in graduation ceremonies for master's degrees. A poet laureate is someone who's been given this distinction.

After the ceremony, there's a lot of feasting and often a sad goodbye to the days of scholarly endeavors—no more burning the midnight oil or striving for literary perfection. This is where the phrase "resting on your laurels" comes from. It means relying on your past successes and not pursuing new challenges or paths to glory. Well, at least for some.... not for authors!

Popularity vs. Profitability

Why does this matter today? As a matter of habit, or maybe just human nature, we are obsessed with competition. As soon as something is invented, right on its heels comes a new kind of award. We just can't seem to stop comparing one thing to another and crowning the moment with a token of our esteem. Ask any Nobel laureate.

And it's fitting, isn't it? What better way to memorialize the moment or benchmark the best? A stroke of genius deserves recognition, whether it's a gold medal in the international Olympic games or a regional award for a new work of fiction. Usually with this recognition comes some kind of remuneration and some amazing publicity opportunities.

We just love to recognize the best, hold it up for example and challenge anyone to do better. It makes for forward progress in the most wonderful way.

This brings us to the topic of book awards and the enormous boost they can give to your reputation—and your book sales.

Top Book Awards List for Authors

Winning an award for your book may seem unlikely at first blush. After all, the competition and requirements for submission are usually thought to be pretty stiff. But in reality, the fee for submitting your magnum opus for Pulitzer Prize consideration is only $50. Some authors spend that amount weekly at their friendly neighborhood Starbucks.

Imagine carrying around the title of "Award-Winning Author" on your business card. You just might get past some velvet ropes a little easier with that kind of clout (hey, it could happen).

Besides Pulitzer and Nobel, the list of prominent book awards reads like a "Who's Who" at an acronym convention: PEN, NBA, NBCC and Booker to name a few. But there are lesser-known, more accessible challenges to meet, such as Benjamin Franklin, Independent Publishers Guild and Writer's Digest. Besides bucking the competition for the major brass rings, you are much more likely to win the Sophomore Cup and be the proverbial big fish in a small pond.

Besides lots of celebratory perks and a cash prize, winners are announced to major trade journals, news outlets, public libraries, social media and blogs. Consider your entry for the following awards when you publish your next manuscript:

The Pulitzer Prize – General Nonfiction: For a distinguished and appropriately documented book of nonfiction by an American author that is not eligible for consideration in any other category.

The Axiom Business Book Awards: The Axiom Business Book Awards are the largest and most respected critical guidepost for business books in today's new world of publishing. These prestigious and competitive awards are presented in 22 business categories and serve as the premier list to help readers discover new and innovative works.

The Benjamin Franklin Awards: The Independent Book Publishers Association is a non-profit organization that offers advocacy and education. Their Benjamin Franklin Award honors independent publishers and self-published authors for excellent book editorial and design.

Independent Publishers Guild Award: The IPG's Independent Publishing Awards celebrate the achievements and successes of IPG members. Frankly, it's a great way for them to drive membership, and it's a great way for you, the author, to connect and network with other serious professionals.

The New Apple Literary Awards for eBooks: New Apple's Annual Summer E-Book Awards was established to honor the creative achievements of the unsung books fighting for their place within the digital publishing world.

Writer's Digest Self-Published eBook Awards: Writer's Digest offers a grand prize of $8,000 and a paid trip to their convention. There are several category prizes of $1,000 each, as well as a free subscription to their magazine.

IPPYS – Independent Publishers Book Awards: The Independent Publisher Book Awards (the IPPYs) shine a light on excellent independent, university, and self-published books each year. The independent spirit comes from all corners, and books are judged on merit, not necessarily polish.

Foreword Magazine Book of the Year Awards: Foreword Reviews is dedicated to discovering new indie books. The INDIEFAB Book of the Year Awards help showcase the best indie books for readers eager to discover new stories by unknown authors.

Dan Poynter Global Book Awards: Winners of this eBook award get the customary hoopla that accompanies book awards—stickers, social media buzz and press releases. As a winner, you'll also be considered for a one-year scholarship award for Dan Poynter's Para Promotion Program.

eLit Awards: The eLit Awards are committed to illuminating and honoring the best of English language entertainment. The eLit Awards include digital publishing in a wide variety of reader formats with submissions from around the world.

Book Reviews: How to Get Book Reviews on Amazon

As an author, the best thing that can happen for your book is that titillating four-letter word we all love and fear at the same time: BUZZ. Getting people to read and talk up your book is what it's all about.

Buzz is the reason for those late nights hunched over your keyboard with an empty cup of something at your elbow, while a long-suffering significant other beckons from the next room to come back to bed. An audience for your greatest ideas is the reason to lie awake, staring at the ceiling, piecing together the right words to express your ideas. Buzz is the reason to take the contents of your head, convert them to verbiage and digits and publish them in an ISBN-backed, endorsement-bedecked, jewel-tone-covered volume called **My Great Work**.

Clearly, buzz is what you want. The goal is to generate a flurry of well-deserved hype over the 3-month timeframe surrounding your book launch and thereby tell the world your story. But how does a lone author working from a spare room get buzz, and how much is enough?

Let's start this question of buzz by addressing the topic of book reviews, or what professional marketers like to refer as Social Proof. There are two types of reviews which authors seek: professional reviews (trade reviews, media outlets, etc.) and consumer reviews. Let's take a deeper look at getting consumer reviews.

Separating the Papyrus from the Chaff

From legacy publishing digests to rogue Indie publishing specialists, information abounds online about how to successfully launch your book and get reviews. After all, consumer book reviews are the bread and butter of many a book launch campaign with good reason. One thing has been proven... consumers make buying decisions based on social proof.

I took a fantastic scuba diving adventure with my daughter, exploring reefs and shipwrecks off the coast of Florida. After seeing the tropical fish in the delightfully warm 86-degree water, Alex, the store manager of the scuba shop, asked us to log into TripAdvisor to write a review. Alex knows how important reviews are to his business—both in terms of positive reviews and the quantity of reviews.

The same principles of getting reviews for a scuba diving shop can be applied to books.

Plenty of quality reviews on Amazon.com alone signals the difference between the roar of the crowd and the figurative chirping of crickets. The average book on Amazon will have less than six reviews. Some marketing tactics require at least 30 reviews on Amazon before you can take your Marketing Plan to the next level. The reason is that several highly effective book marketing tactics require that you have this number before you can launch a substantial campaign.

So, what are the steps you can add to your marketing checklist to kick-off your book launch with lots of reviews?

The 5 Most Effective Steps You Can Take to Get More Book Reviews

1. **Develop an overall Marketing Plan.** Think about how you can market your book as you're writing it—not as an afterthought. If you wait until your manuscript

is finished, you will either delay the launch or suffer from low book sales. Include book reviews as part of this plan, and draft a clear, specific strategy for getting them.

2. **Write a great book.** The book you write should stand up to thoughtful analysis, whether it's fiction or non-fiction. Have it professionally edited, commission an excellent cover and let your book stand on its own merits.

3. **Keep a list of reviewers.** Develop and organize a list of people to tap for reviews as you're writing your book. Ask yourself, "Who has a vested interest in expressing their opinion about my work?" Begin this task early on, and maintain steady activity. Here are a few ideas to get started building your list:

   – Friends and Family: Reach out to your inner circle of people closest to you and ask for a favor to write a review once your book is published. Some authors can achieve the requisite 30 reviews from this source alone.

   – Fans and Supporters: Keep a list of people who know, like and trust you. These folks will have the greatest emotional investment in the success of your book. Many authors will organize a "book launch tribe" who perform various tasks throughout the book launch. Using social media networks is an excellent forum for organizing tribe members.

   – Colleagues: List the people who are in your industry who would be interested in supporting your work.

You can trade promotion with them and perhaps even launch a joint venture promotion.

- Reviewers: These are people who have an established reputation in the field of literary criticism. This category includes book bloggers, media personnel and celebrities. Notable reviewers can be your most effective allies in getting attention for your book.

- Podcasters: Remember podcasting? Team up with podcasters to review your book and help you spread the word. Better yet, recommend that they tie their review to a 3-part series that includes an interview with you and a retrospective on your topic. The more you prepare material for them, the greater the chances of success for both of you.

- Online Retail Communities: Request book reviews on from top reviewers on Amazon.com, GoodReads.com, iTunes, BarnesandNoble.com and other similar e-tailers. Be polite, be informative, and follow up. Finding these reviewers is easier than you think... keep reading.

4. **Get engaged.** Cultivate relationships with the people you want to review your work. Be willing to trade your engagement with them for their thoughtful comments about your book. Be ready to get involved in their conversations on their blogs and social media. Participate. In this area, the more attention you give, the more attention you will receive.

5. **Get social.** Use social media to generate excitement about your work in progress. Don't just release your book—launch it. As your big day approaches, make

it clear that advance copies of your book are available in exchange for credible reviews. The number of copies you give away will have a marked impact on the number of reviews you receive. However, scarcity sells. Position the review copies as a scarce commodity, even when you're giving away a thousand of them. In fact, expert review campaigns in advance of your book launch can lead to best-seller status for your book. I've seen it happen time and again. Promoting review copies on social media is a great way to jump-start your campaign.

Getting quality book reviews isn't rocket science, and it doesn't have to keep you up at night. After all, those long hours spent staring at the ceiling are best kept for crafting your magnum opus. Using these five steps will make your book promotion that much easier and help you get the kind of buzz you're looking for. The right reviews at the right time can be just the nudge you need.

Sample Campaign – The Tried and True Book Selling Technique

Now that you're paying attention to how books are marketed, there's no doubt you've witnessed other authors racing to the top of the best-seller charts, and you wonder what they're doing to build mega success. If you're like most authors, you're not sure how to go about reaping this kind of success for yourself.

Want to know a secret? You don't have to be original to be good.

In fact, the less original you are in some cases, the better off you'll be. As they say, success leaves tracks. Follow the tracks, and you'll find success.

Take for example the traditional author's boring, stalwart best friend, the Sample Campaign. Sending samples of your book to retail buyers, bloggers, reviewers and other influencers will boost awareness with the people who matter most, gaining exposure for your book and for you as an author. Using giveaways to create buzz while you are in pre-launch can be an inexpensive and effective way to generate publicity.

The Sample Campaign involves sending either physical copies of your book to reviewers or distributing e-copies to qualified centers of influence. Both tactics involve an investment of time, research, risk and reward.

Launching a Sample Campaign may sound expensive— and it is expensive if you try to get creative with this approach, but there are ways you can be both unoriginal and highly successful.

Copycat Book Marketing and Other Cheats

If you're going to model the best, start by looking at the Amazon best seller list within your book's category. Find the best-selling books that are most like yours, and model their marketing tactics. What do you see? Would you buy these best sellers?

The odds are high that all of these books have received the royal treatment from a staff of pros, yet the approach is kept focused and simple.

What best-selling authors know is that the goal is to get attention from centers of influence. People who have a megaphone and a crowd who are always glad to lend an opinion.

If you want to get lots of good reviews from your Sample Campaign, you've got to make your book buzzworthy. Make sure it's not just a scintillating read, but engaging from the first moment readers encounter it.

First Impressions: The title, book cover and description are the most influential elements when it comes to helping people determine whether or not they will buy your book—or review it for their audience.

Professional Design: Your book cover is the most important feature of your book, and it should be intriguing. Make sure your cover is a match for your genre. If you've written a mystery, don't use romance imagery—the kind with windswept lovers embracing on a naked rock above a storm-wracked cove. You might raise an eyebrow or two, but where's the mystery? A poor cover will make it harder to sell your book.

Enticing Description: Your description needs to pull people in as well. Start your description with something provocative, and use your chosen keywords right up front. Make buyers and reviewers ravenous for more. Would you buy your book if you read your own description?

How Can You Distribute Sample Copies of Your Book?

Review copies are given away free, but that doesn't mean they shouldn't come at a price for the reviewer. Select only reviewers who are the most likely to come through with their promised action. Because you will be investing your time, resources and energy in distributing your samples, be choosy about who gets to have them.

Here is a 3-step formula to generate heat in your Sample Campaign, used by marketing pros who are "in the know" about how to sell books.

Step 1: Goodreads Setup. You already know about Goodreads. com from a previous chapter, but many authors use an ineffective approach. Start by creating a reader account using your author name. Before you do anything else, get familiar with the venue (this is called "lurking"), then review several books. After you've become a trusted member of the community, you can add your book or have someone add it for you.

Once your book has been added, you can change your status to "author." You'll have to submit an application to Goodreads' staff for review, and this takes a couple of days. Be sure to add your social media links to your Goodreads account and website.

Once you're established on Goodreads.com, click the link to "Create A Giveaway." These are physical books you're giving away, so you'll need to buy copies of your book and send them to the reviewers who request it. Be sure you conduct only one giveaway at a time, or this can get expensive and confusing.

Step 2: Blog Tours. Capitalizing on blog tours is an excellent cog in the wheel of your Sample Campaign. To do this, take a title from your Kindle best seller list and Google it with the search term "blog tour." This search will yield bloggers who customarily review books and need something to blog about.

Your next step is to contact the bloggers and ask them if they would be interested in reviewing your book. Give them plenty of advance notice; typically about two months. Popular reviewers are often booked well in advance, and these are the ones you want to reach.

When you contact them, include a link to your Goodreads page so they can see your alluring cover and intriguing book description. Ask for their review to be published within the first five days of your release, preferably on your actual release date.

Step 3: Brick and Mortar. Indie bookstores love authors, and many would welcome you for an author book signing. When you run your giveaway campaign, contact the store manager first before you seed the marketplace with copies of your book. Make it your goal to send out only copies that will actually yield results. Track where each one goes and follow up until you get solid results.

If you work with a publisher, ask them for a list of buyers from their Rolodex to send samples.

Book reviewers are real people with busy lives. When you request a review, don't make the mistake of pitching your book like a used car salesman. A brief personal introduction followed by a simple paragraph describing your book should do the trick. Ask for permission to send them a review copy, and then be sure to follow up. Stay on track until you achieve the success you're seeking. Some reviewers will request a PDF of your manuscript, while others will insist on receiving a physical copy of the book.

With this kind of focused activity, perhaps someday you will find your work on the best seller list... and start reaping the success your literary endeavor deserves!

Trade Publication Reviews and Big Exposure

Of all the tactics an author can use to become noteworthy, getting your book reviewed by the *New York Times* is right up there.

A thumbs up from the likes of *Publishers Weekly* or the *Library Journal* is not just some stroke for the author's ego. It can translate to big bucks in terms of buy-in for your book. The right recommendation can open doors for an author where before there only seemed to be a brick wall.

Once you've finished writing your book, getting wide distribution in the marketplace should naturally become your focus. Book buyers hesitate to engage with an author they've never heard of. I mean, even you and I hover briefly over the *1-Click Order* button on Amazon before committing to an unknown author. Book buyers and readers alike look for a source of information they can trust before making a buying decision on a book in a sea of millions of book titles.

Reviews provide that confirmation, whether the comments come from consumers or professional critics. So, let's explore how to get your book reviewed by major trade publications. Every successful author has been unknown at some point, and reviews help to bridge that gap between obscurity and celebrity. Finding reviewers who are willing make your name known is a simpler process than you might expect.

Why Book-Trade Reviews?

Reviews have a permanence that time-based media just doesn't have. TV and radio shows can offer a wide audience. However, their time-based quality means a lot less leverage for you, the author, in getting your name in front of your chosen audience. The shows typically air just once, and then they're gone.

Written reviews in trade journals, libraries, magazines and websites will last for years. Any time your book-buying public is looking for information about you or your topic, they're going to stumble across those reviews. In fact, you can even excerpt these reviews and use them in your marketing materials.

So how do you do it? What's the secret to getting the guys at the top to notice you? Is there some kind of mojo that only hired publicists have the license to practice? Let's look at a two-pronged effort to do just that.

Freedom of the Press and Other Juicy Tactics

One method you can use to publicize your book is writing press releases and getting distribution. Sometimes press releases are picked up by major publications, which can provide amazing support for a book release.

In addition to reprints from major media outlets, your press release can end up being indexed by Google for your main keywords. This puts your announcement in front of all kinds of book reviewers, online bloggers and the buying public.

To request a book review from one of the major trade publications, the process is not that complicated. In fact, it involves only one step: **ask**.

Start by sending a personalized e-mail with details about your book, then wait for a response. Make your query tailored to the publication you're submitting it to, and use the editor's name in your greeting. Don't make your submission about you; make it about them. Be direct about how your material will interest and benefit their audience.

This method may yield a certain amount of failures, but that's part of the process. The best baseball player hits the ball only 3 out of 10 times. You can make up for what you lack in skill with a large number of review submissions. And over time, you'll get better.

With that in mind, here is a list of contacts for Media & Trade Review Submissions:

Foreword Reviews: A paid review service, respected throughout the industry. Great to post on retailer websites, such as Amazon's Editorial Review.

New York Times: Getting your book reviewed by the *New York Times* can have a material impact on your sales.

Publishers Weekly: Respected source of book reviews, circulated to trade book buyers. If you are working with a Publisher on your book release, it is recommended that they help with this submission. And here's a professional tip—a little advertising for your book in Publishers Weekly might be just the ticket to rise above the noise.

Library Journal: Oriented to librarians, with great influence in the library industry. Again, this is another source of professional reviews that might be best to run through your Publisher.

Kirkus: A paid review service, geared to indie authors.

Shelf Awareness: These reviews are circulated to retail trade buyers and are exceptional sources of awareness for a book release.

Booklist: Book review site geared towards public and school libraries. Also used by many book clubs.

New York Review of Books: Billed as *the premier literary-intellectual magazine in the English language.*

Choice: Geared to meet the needs of undergraduate students, this is considered the premier site for reviews of academic books.

The hardest part of putting your book in front of the professionals on this list is getting started. It can be overwhelming. Contacting any publication you respect or admire can be intimidating. So muster-up your courage and dive in. Get organized, and keep moving.

Remember that reviewers would be out of business if it weren't for authors like you. You have an obligation to give them something to talk about. Who knows? The next review you read may be your own!

11

The All-Important
Pre-Order Campaign

ONCE all the components of your book marketing plan have been identified, organized and implemented, it is time to work on getting your fans to pre-order the book with major retailers. The quantity of pre-orders in retailers like Amazon can result in massive follow-up book orders. Know that other retailers such as Target.com & WalMart.com also keep a close eye on book pre-orders and the quantity of pre-orders in their system can inform their in-store merchandising decisions.

With this nugget of information, let's unpack the details of running a pre-order campaign.

How to Set Up a Book Pre-Order Campaign

Talking about books sometimes takes me to interesting places... like picturesque Ashland, Oregon, for instance. On a recent trip, the topic of generating pre-orders for new book releases came up over lunch. Here is how the conversation developed...

Ashland sits in the heart of the up-and-coming wine country of Southern Oregon, and it's long been home to the famous Ashland Shakespeare Festival. Wine and words—an undoubtedly winning combination in my book. I'm sure the Bard himself would have approved of this fabulous business lunch with an executive of our audiobook distribution team among the cobblestones and Tudor half-timbers.

As my colleague and I sat in a quaint bistro on a glorious afternoon—talking about library orders, taking in the crisp air, and observing the bustle of college students on the streets below—I looked over the menu with a critical case of indecision. Everything looked so delicious. Just as I was about to make my choice, our server sauntered over and filled us in on the specials.

She quietly mentioned that the Crab Newburg was sold out. "There's a big family reunion here tonight," she explained. "They've pre-ordered the entire right side of the menu."

Suddenly, I had a mouthwatering desire for Crab Newburg with an insistency that cannot be explained. But no matter the desire, there was no way to satisfy my appetite for the buttery little delights. I settled for the chicken fettuccine served with a smattering of prosciutto and capers (yawn!). As the conversation developed, the executive I was meeting with began explaining the incredible importance of generating pre-orders in major retail catalogs for new book releases. In that moment, everything came together and it all made sense.

There's a new dynamic in the book publishing world, she explained, and it directly affects our new authors. Here is what she dished out while I poked at my plate of poultry.

Many authors will run a pre-sales marketing campaign for their book release. This sends a signal to retail buyers about the number of readers who are eager for the upcoming launch. One factor that dictates how many books a retailer will buy up-front is the number of pre-orders they see in their system for the new release.

Having pre-orders can mean the difference between big retailers like Barnes & Noble or Amazon ordering, say, 400 units of your book versus 2,000 units. In other words, it's the difference between having a pedestrian chicken dish, or landing an exotic Pacific Northwest crustacean delicacy served with a piquant cream sauce and a splash of dry sherry. One tries; the other succeeds.

I should mention that my lunch partner is an executive with direct working experience with Barnes & Noble, Baker & Taylor, and Books a Million, along with an impressive number of libraries. She was very clear on the topic of getting pre-orders of your book and emphasized it as a major priority. More than ever, book buyers look at the following hot topics when ordering for their stores and libraries:

- How famous is the author?

- How do the book Title and cover artwork work together?

- What is the author's marketing plan for this book?

- How many book pre-orders are in their system?

If you have intentions of succeeding in the hyper-competitive retail book business, here is what savvy authors are doing to stimulate pre-orders for their book release, which we call the **Seven Step Pre-order Campaign**:

1. Build a page on your website with at least five links to pre-order books. This signals retail buyers that you are not partial to any single retailer.

2. Include links to your book on a variety of retail websites. Here is a suggested list (providing your publisher has distribution with these retailers):

   a. Amazon

   b. BarnesandNoble.com

   c. Target

   d. WalMart

   e. Books a Million

   f. IndieBound

3. Send messages to your fans via social media and email broadcasts. Try live streaming video options which are getting impressive response rates.

4. Offer a bonus item to your fans for placing pre-orders, such as free digital content. A PDF or MP3 audio file is often popular. Have people message you with a digital receipt of their retail order to get the bonus offer.

5. Offer to sign their book if they mail it to you with return postage. It can be some extra work, but it tells your fans that you care.

6. Give away a coupon code for a free copy of your digital audiobook.

7. Encourage people to write a review where they purchased the book.

For maximum distribution from your publishing supply chain, make sure that a pre-order campaign is on your menu. In several cases, a successful pre-order campaign has resulted in the sell-out of the initial print run of books, so keep a close eye on your results. Stay in close communications with your Publisher on your activities and help smooth out any surprises. This one marketing tactic which can ensure your book sales are as fresh as today's fresh catch!

12

How to Pay
for Your Book Launch

HAVING worked with hundreds of authors, it is a well-known fact that authors have limited time and budget to allocate to promoting a book release. If you do not have enough time to run your own marketing campaign, then let's explore the option of getting your campaign funded so someone else can manage these details.

There are common methods of funding a marketing campaign without digging into your own pocket. These unusual sources of revenue to pay for a book campaign are within reach, and in this section, we can explore if any are right for you.

Top 4 Methods for Funding a Book Marketing Campaign

1. **Sell a corporate sponsorship:** If your book is a good fit, some corporations may choose to pay for advertising or sponsorship of your book. For instance, if you are writing a book about essential oils, the manufacturers of essential oils may be very interested in sponsoring your book in order to get exposure for their line of essential oils. For the corporate sponsor, exposure to thousands, tens of thousands or hundreds of thousands of readers is incredibly valuable real estate!

2. **Run a pre-order campaign:** Some authors will run a pre-order campaign before their book releases, and offer incentives to pre-order books. Authors who choose this approach have paid for their book campaign in full, just from pre-orders. This approach does imply that you have an existing "tribe" or group of fans who are motivated to place orders prior to your release date.

3. **Joint Venture Affiliate Marketing Campaign:** A popular method of paying for your book release is to recruit a network of affiliates who will earn a percent of your sales in exchange for promoting your book. Here are a variety of structures to consider using when running a Joint Venture campaign:

   - Free copy of your book, when people pay for shipping.

   - Register the purchase receipt number from other retailers (like Amazon or Barnes & Noble) on your website, then send a free offer. You can send valuable video resources, research, white papers or other valuable intellectual property.

- Free gift with purchase when people order with you directly.

- When a buyer completes an order for your book, then offer an Upsell Offer. After the purchase of a book, an upsell can be priced between $47 and $197, and can be valued at $97-$197—which sometimes includes limited access to the author. Consider offering a 30-minute phone consultation where readers can ask questions directly with the expert.

- The upsell offer can convert at a rate of 10% of book buyers. This is important to know, because you need to provide a financial incentive for the Affiliates to promote your book release to their lists. A professional Affiliate Marketer will ask you about your conversion rates before agreeing to this style of campaign, so it makes sense to run some tests prior to talking to Affiliates.

4. **Run a Crowd Funding Campaign:** This is a popular method for raising funds for a book launch. Let's explore this idea in more detail in this case study from a successful book launch campaign.

Case Study
Funding a Book Launch with Kickstarter

Imagine yourself on a vast playing field in a sports stadium—a dream from childhood come true. The turf you're standing on is a rich emerald green under the bright stadium lights. For a brief moment, you're in awe that you've finally made it big as you scan the thousands of faces cheering you on.

The stands are filled to capacity—more than 65,000 souls—and the roar of the crowd is all but deafening with only seconds left in the game. You and your teammates have been moving like a well-oiled machine, playing all-out the entire game. Now it's down to the wire. The other team is pushing hard to score, but you and your crew shut them down just in time. The game is over, and victory is yours!

What an amazing feeling to aim for something and hit the mark. This is true not only in sports, but in business and life as well. When you set a goal and commit to it, all kinds of strange, happy coincidences conspire to bring you what you've decided upon.

Author Michael Tetteh knows first-hand just how true this is. Michael had that experience just described, playing professional soccer for the wildly popular Seattle Sounders. It was his fondest dream, as a nine-year-old boy living in Ghana, to play professional soccer.

Michael's journey from a humble African village to living the life of a sports celebrity in a major U.S. city only happened because he'd taken that first step—setting a goal. He followed his dream and used his natural gifts to become a successful soccer player.

Michael is now retired from the sport and has written an account of his unique and glamorous story. His book, *Giftocracy*, is based on the idea that everyone has a gift—a unique talent that when channeled, is your unique path to success. Michael set a goal to raise money to cover the marketing costs of his book launch. How did he accomplish this? He used the Crowdfunding Website Kickstarter.

Reaching Your Goal with Kickstarter

Kickstarter is a huge worldwide community of like-minded people offering each other support. The website's mission is to help artists, authors, performers and other creative people. It's a platform where everyday people can raise the money needed to reach creative goals. Since Kickstarter's launch in 2009, the site has helped over 12 million people fund a project. More than 115,562 projects have been funded, with a total of $2.7 billion pledged.

In my travels around the globe talking to authors, the topic of funding a book release came up during a discussion with an author. She asked if I knew anything about crowdfunding generally, and Kickstarter specifically. I shared that if she raised $25,000 to fund her book project, then she would have the budget to launch a healthy marketing campaign to gain nationwide attention to her ideas.

As you might imagine, my client was enthusiastic and wanted to get started right away. Here are four steps to fund a book launch with Kickstarter.

1. **Amount:** Determine your fundraising goal. Here are some thoughts to get you started:

   a. Raise $7,000 - 10,000 to self-publish your book, including graphic design and layout.

   b. Raise $20,000 - $40,000 to work with an experienced ghostwriter.

   c. Raise $25,000 - $50,000 to plan a robust marketing launch complete with a professional publicist to schedule a media tour

   d. Raise $250,000 if your aspirations are to run a marketing campaign that will produce a New York Times bestseller.

2. **Appeal:** Create excellent visual photography assets to represent your book or your ideas. You'll need these for your Kickstarter project page so people can see what they're buying into. You'll also want to record a thoughtful, heartfelt or funny video about your project—about 3 to 7 minutes long. You want to move people and get them excited about supporting your cause. Besides using photos and video, Kickstarter Live is an option to stream live video of your appeal.

3. **Bonuses:** Create an inventory of bonuses that you will give away with each level of donation. Here is an example of how a Business author might structure their giveaway.

   a. $10 for a copy of the eBook and a custom mug.

   b. $25 for a pre-release signed copy of your book.

   c. $50 for a 5-pack of signed books for your staff.

    d. $100 for a nice gift item, with a copy of your book.

    e. $250 for a nicer gift item, with a copy of your book.

    f. $1,000 for an event such as a dinner for four with the author.

    g. $5,000 for a free speaking engagement to an organization of your choice (charity event, fund raiser, corporate retreat or another gathering).

4. **Communicate:** Write good copy for your landing page. In fact, unless you have a marketing degree, hire a professional to write your copy for you. Your writing needs to pack a punch. Then once you launch your campaign, talk it up! Tell your friends and promote the campaign in your social circles. Know that it takes several reminders to fund a campaign fully. You'll want to be active on social media and send plenty of emails. Many successful authors even pick up the phone (gasp) to personally ask people to support their campaigns.

When you start thinking like a professional fundraiser, you'll do great! When people like your Kickstarter project, they love to join your journey and see it as a joy to support your cause. Remember to thank them for that precious support and then follow-up when your project is complete with a hand-written note.

Conclusion

CONGRATULATIONS! Now that you've read this book, I would like to welcome you to an elite class of authors in the top 2% of the world. You are now educated on how to market a book, but are also aware of the details of managing the smartest book marketing tactics on the market.

For the authors who can check off everything on this list, you are embarking on the rarified territory of becoming a #1 Best Seller!

Candidly, most authors who exercise a book launch campaign to this level of detail have typically published 3-6 books, developed through an arduous series of trial and error campaigns. If you are working on your first book, then you are far ahead of the curve with this knowledge.

The work outlined in this book is what publishing insiders call **Platform**, and is your ticket to many advantages, whether it be landing a traditional publishing deal or generating a generous return on your book launch.

While you are in your 15-week launch mode, keep this material close to your workspace as this advice can produce tremendous results along your path to a successful book launch.

Good selling! We look forward to seeing your book on the best-seller list!

Appendix

The Book Marketing Prioritization System

THROUGH years of counseling ambitious speakers and authors, the Book Marketing Prioritization System has emerged with an ideal mix of book marketing tactics to include in a book marketing campaign. This system is designed by a professional book marketing team—one who has tested and discarded marketing tactics for over a decade in order to compile the most effective list of marketing activities possible.

But it is also understood that not everyone has the kind of time needed to do all these activities. Therefore, this system was created to help visualize the most effective marketing tactics from a high level. Each item in this table has been indexed on a system based on effectiveness divided by cost. We want you to be able to clearly see the most effective marketing activities, relative to how much it may cost or how much time it takes to perform. Hence, this will help you identify which activities are the best spend of your time and budget.

One author Pat Hawks who was very successful with her bookstore tour was quoted as saying "I love checklists." As such, here is a checklist you can use that takes the process one step further by identifying the ideal timing in which to perform each of these marketing activities.

Each marketing tactic is listed in terms of the number of weeks prior to your book launch, as to the ideal time to be focused on each task. If you organize each week during this 15-week timeframe, this system will act as the ideal guideline to structure your activity.

With years of experience in book marketing, this checklist also has a handy "Effectiveness Index," which will help you prioritize which activities are the most important based on tracking years of historical data on book marketing. The Effectiveness Index is a blend between time cost and monetary cost, in terms of how effective each tactic is in selling books. Any activity that earned an index over 100% is highly recommended activity for your personal checklist.

15 Week Book Marketing Checklist

✓	Book Marketing Ideas	Overview	Effectiveness Index	15-Week Checklist
	Marketing Plan	Draft a written marketing plan for the launch of your book.	200%	Week 15
	Article Inventory	Create an inventory of articles and post on a period basis.	100%	Week 15
	Kickstarter Campaign	Run a Kickstarter. com campaign to fund your marketing campaign and book inventory needs.	167%	Week 15
	Awards & Writing Contests	Submit manuscript for writing awards & contests.	200%	Week 15
	Branding & Positioning	Finding your Voice in the marketplace. Includes Brainstorm, Case Studies, Core Values, Mission Statement, Positioning Statement, Moniker.	133%	Week 14
	Author Bio	Create 3 author Bios: 25 words, 100 words, 250 words	100%	Week 14

✓	Book Marketing Ideas	Overview	Effectiveness Index	15-Week Checklist
	Photography	Hire a professional photographer to get a series of headshots & speaker poses. TIP: have your photographer shoot pictures that are consistent with your Brand image.	50%	Week 14
	Endorsements	Request 10 endorsements from high profile people/celebrities/authors.	300%	Week 14
	Social Media Activity	Create social media accounts and build an inventory of posts to circulate on a regular basis. Include image inventory for future posts.	100%	Week 13
	Keyword Inventory	Think through keywords that people will search on Google which have to do with your book topic. Keep an inventory. Consider working with a pro to research keyword phrases.	200%	Week 12
	Virtual Assistant	Hire a VA to manage the details and timing of your Marketing Plan.	33%	Week 12
	Website (book website and/or speaker website)	Build a web presence for yourself or your book.	67%	Week 12

✓	Book Marketing Ideas	Overview	Effectiveness Index	15-Week Checklist
	Paid Placement with National Chains (airport stores, etc.)	Guaranteed "featured display" for X-days with National Accounts.	125%	Week 12
	Media Kit	Build a media kit for news outlets.	200%	Week 12
	Speaker One-Sheet	One-page summary of Keynote speech.	50%	Week 12
	Speaking Lead Research Study	Research to build a list of targeted leads for speaking engagements.	150%	Week 11
	Press Release	Develop a press "angle," write & circulate a series of press releases.	200%	Week 11
	Book Trailer Video	Highly produced video promoting the book.	67%	Week 11
	Product Funnel	Build the perfect product funnel to monetize the leads generated from books/speaking.	133%	Week 11
	Blog Tour	Research high traffic blogs and request to become a contributor.	250%	Week 10
	Contact Local Radio & TV	Prepare newsworthy story angles.	300%	Week 10
	Contact Local Newsprint/ Magazine	Prepare newsworthy articles & submit as a regular contributor.	250%	Week 10
	Influencer Magazines	Submit request to become a regular contributor to prestigious print publications.	150%	Week 9

✓	Book Marketing Ideas	Overview	Effectiveness Index	15-Week Checklist
	Book Poster	Book poster to promote the book.	50%	Week 8
	Bookmarks	Bookmarks to give away, promoting the benefits of your book.	50%	Week 8
	LinkedIn Groups	Sign-up for relevant groups on Linkedin and become an "active" voice in the community. Stay relevant.	200%	Week 7
	HARO PR	Subscribe to HARO (free daily PR resource called Help a Reporter Out). This resource enables you to pitch story ideas to reporters who are hungry for your expertise.	400%	Week 7
	Goodreads	Create a Goodreads account and become active in the community as a Reader and as an Author.	200%	Week 6
	Video Marketing Campaign	Record a series of videos & post to social networks (YouTube, Facebook, LinkedIn).	67%	Week 6
	5 Local Networking Events Per Month	Relevant networking, getting out into the public with your message.	100%	Week 6

✓	Book Marketing Ideas	Overview	Effectiveness Index	15-Week Checklist
	Develop List of Influencers	Locate key players for potential Joint Venture Partners to assist in book release.	500%	Week 6
	Amazon Author Central Account	Set-up your Amazon Author Central Account and link to your blog & social accounts.	100%	Week 6
	"Review" Campaign	Plan a campaign to encourage Reviews on Amazon/ Goodreads/iTunes/ B&N. Target getting a minimum of 30 Reviews on Amazon. TIP: Some authors choose to release their ebook prior to their physical book to get consumer reviews in advance of their physical book release date.	167%	Week 5
	Promotions	Run promotional campaigns to draw attention to your book such as sweepstakes & giveaways.	150%	Week 5
	Corporate Outreach	Sales calls to key corporate clients (send a sample of your book & a bulk order form).	167%	Week 4
	Email List broadcasts	List Building and Email Broadcasts to warm-up your prospects.	50%	Week 4

✓	Book Marketing Ideas	Overview	Effectiveness Index	15-Week Checklist
	Webinars	Speaking/discussing key principles from the book.	100%	Week 4
	Goodreads Giveaways	Run a series of book giveaways to raise awareness.	100%	Week 4
	Ad Campaigns	Purchase banner advertising on Goodreads, Amazon, Facebook, Google, BookBub, etc.	100%	Week 4
	SEO	Top search engine rankings by promoting keywords in articles.	100%	Week 3
	Bestseller Campaign	Target sending 500,000 to 2 million email broadcast day-of-launch with a series of Joint Venture partners.	100%	Week 2
	Tell a Friend Campaign	Offer an incentive to consumers to tell their friends about a book.	150%	Week 1
	Book Launch Party	Organize an event around your book launch. Invite Influencers and local media.	150%	Week 0
	BookBub Campaign	Promote a 5-day ebook price promotion (free, $.99, $1.99 or $2.99) from high performing site BookBub.	200%	Week 0

About Author

BRYAN **Heathman** is the CEO of Made for Success Publishing and the author of Conversion Marketing: Convert Website Visitors into Buyers. Bryan's Fortune 500 marketing career includes companies with powerful brands including Microsoft, Eastman Kodak Company and Xerox.

With hundreds of marketing campaigns to his credit, Bryan's marketing advice is sought-out by authors worldwide. Visit Bryan at BryanHeathman.com.